what is this thing called metaphysics?

Second edition

Why is there something rather than nothing? Does God exist? Does time flow? What are we? Do we have free will? What is truth? Metaphysics is concerned with ourselves and reality, and the most fundamental questions regarding existence. This clear and accessible introduction covers the central topics in metaphysics in a concise but comprehensive way. Brian Garrett discusses the crucial concepts in a highly readable manner, easing the reader in with a look at some important philosophical problems. He addresses key areas of metaphysics:

- God
- Existence
- Modality
- Universals and particulars
- Facts
- Puzzles of material constitution
- Causation
- Time
- Free will
- Personal identity
- Truth

This second edition has been thoroughly revised. Most chapters have substantial amounts of new material, and there are additional chapters on Existence, Modality, Puzzles of Material Constitution, Facts and Truth.

What is this thing called Metaphysics? contains many helpful student-friendly features. Each chapter concludes with a useful summary of the main ideas discussed, a glossary of important terms, study questions, annotated further reading, and a guide to web resources. Text boxes provide bite-sized summaries of key concepts and major philosophers, and clear and interesting examples are used throughout.

Brian Garrett is Senior Lecturer in Philosophy at the Australian National University, Australia.

BRIAN GARRETT

what is this thing called metaphysics?

Second edition

Routledge
Taylor & Francis Group

LONDON AND NEW YORK

First published 2006
This edition published 2011 by Routledge
2 Park Square, Milton Park, Abingdon, Oxon, OX14 4RN

Simultaneously published in the USA and Canada
by Routledge
711 Third Avenue, New York, NY 10017

Routledge is an imprint of the Taylor & Francis Group, an informa business

The right of Brian Garrett to be identified as author of this work has been
asserted by him in accordance with sections 77 and 78 of the Copyright,
Designs and Patents Act 1988.

Typeset in Berling and Arial Rounded by
Saxon Graphics Ltd, Derby
Printed and bound in Great Britain by
TJ International Ltd, Padstow, Cornwall

British Library Cataloguing in Publication Data
A catalogue record for this book is available from the British Library

Library of Congress Cataloging in Publication Data
Garrett, Brian.
What is this thing called metaphysics?/Brian Garrett. – 2nd ed.
p. cm.
Includes bibliographical references and index.
1. Metaphysics. I. Title.

BD111.G37 2011
110--dc22
2010040857

ISBN: 978-0-415-61721-5 (hbk)
ISBN: 978-0-415-61722-2 (pbk)
ISBN: 978-0-203-82623-2 (ebk)

'Well, you see Willard ... In this war, things get confused out there, power, ideals, the old morality, and practical military necessity. Out there with these natives it must be a temptation to be god. Because there's a conflict in every human heart between the rational and the irrational, between good and evil. The good does not always triumph. Sometimes the dark side overcomes what Lincoln called the better angels of our nature. Every man has got a breaking point. You and I have. Walter Kurtz has reached his. And very obviously, he has gone insane.'

General Corman, Apocalypse Now (1979)

CONTENTS

PREFACE TO THE FIRST EDITION

I began writing this book during a sabbatical from the Australian National University (ANU) in the first half of 2005. I am grateful to ANU for the leave from teaching. In subsequent seminars at ANU, working through draft chapters, I received useful feedback from my colleagues. Thanks especially to Jeremy Shearmur and Peter Roeper, but also to Havi Carel and Udo Thiel. Thanks also to those graduate students who attended the seminars: David Wall, Peter Grundy, Peter Eldridge-Smith, Luc Small, Paul Miller and Matt Cox.

I'm grateful to Routledge's Philosophy Editor, Tony Bruce, for his encouragement; to Priyanka Pathak, the Development Editor, for her advice and comments; and to Tim Crane for putting me in touch with Tony. I made a number of revisions as a result of critical feedback from three Routledge referees. In addition, my former student Robert Nichols wielded his editorial pen with characteristic incisiveness; John Gregory cast a civil servant's eye over the entire text; and Thomas Mautner allowed me to draw on his extensive knowledge of the history of philosophy.

In an attempt to make the book as user-friendly as possible, Routledge suggested the format whereby each chapter is replete with concept boxes, philosopher profiles, key quotes, glossed words, study questions, further reading, and Internet resources. Hopefully, the reader will find these useful. But if some key words and phrases are still unclear, I warmly recommend Thomas Mautner's *Dictionary of Philosophy* (second edition, London: Penguin, 2005) as an indispensable aid to further understanding.

PREFACE TO THE SECOND EDITION

I am grateful to Adam Johnson and Tony Bruce for giving me the opportunity to revise this for a second edition. It has turned out to be a complete re-write, with a lot of new material. I have added four new chapters and significantly revised most of the remaining ones. I hope it is better for it. A number of people have provided feedback on earlier drafts. Thanks are due to: Daniel Stoljar, Thomas Mautner, Denis Robinson, Harold Noonan, Daniel Nolan, Katrina Hutchison, Jonathan Farrell, Bruin Christensen and J J Joaquin. Let me also express my gratitude to the two Routledge referees for very useful comments.

INTRODUCTION

In ancient and medieval times, metaphysics was conceived as the science which investigates 'being *qua* being' or 'the first causes of things' or 'things that do not change'. On this conception, the metaphysician is concerned to investigate the most general and ubiquitous features of reality, and to uncover the most fundamental principles that apply to everything that is real.

On a more modest conception, the task of the metaphysician is to delineate our most basic or fundamental concepts and chart the various inter-connections between them. The concepts studied (e.g., concepts of time, space, cause, self) are those that any rational being would need to employ in order to make sense of their experience of the world around them. Metaphysics, on this view, is an investigation into that 'massive central core of human thinking which has no history' (P.F. Strawson, *Individuals*, 1959).

Both conceptions of metaphysics are tenable, but the approach taken in this book conforms to the more ambitious conception.

In Chapter 1 we examine the three traditional arguments for God's existence – the Ontological, Cosmological and Teleological arguments, respectively. The discussion introduces and makes use of the notions of contingency and necessity, in particular the idea of a **necessary being**. The Ontological and Teleological arguments are open to effective criticism, but the Cosmological Argument is harder to refute. The chapter ends by discussing the question: given all the worlds that might have existed and been inhospitable to life, why does the world that actually exists allow for life?

In Chapter 2 we attempt to answer a fundamental question: what are we? A range of theories of our nature and identity are subjected to scrutiny. All major theories – Dualism, Animalism, Humeanism and Constitutionalism – are found to be open to objection.

In Chapter 3 we are concerned not with what exists, but with what it is to exist. Is existence a property of ordinary objects? Does my desk have the properties of being wooden, brown, four-legged and existing? To answer 'yes' is to endorse the property view of existence. Those who defend this view tend to embrace the doctrine that there are non-existent objects. These are objects which possess many properties, but not the property of existence. There are many problems with this doctrine and, like the property view, it should be rejected.

In Chapter 4 we look at issues to do with **metaphysical possibility** and **necessity**. Objects and **natural kinds** have essential properties; some truths are necessary, others

contingent. How are we to account for these **modal** facts? Some philosophers (most famously W.V.O. Quine) have doubted the coherence of essentialism, and questioned standard assumptions about the distinction between necessary and contingent truths. We evaluate these doubts. Various theories of necessary truth have been advanced, the most extreme of which is David Lewis's modal **realism**. This theory, along with others, is outlined and criticized.

In Chapter 5 we look at various puzzles concerning the constitution and identity of artefacts. Is a statue identical to the lump of clay which constitutes it? Can a ship survive the removal and replacement of all its planks? If it can, and if the removed planks are used to construct a replica of the original ship, which of the two later ships is the original? In answering these questions, we look at two dominant theories of the identity of objects over time – endurantist and perdurantist theories – and assess the different ways they deal with these puzzles.

In Chapter 6 we are concerned with the nature of properties, but also with the nature of objects. Are properties universals, identical in their instances, as realists believe? Or should we be **nominalists** and hold that properties can be understood without appeal to universals – e.g., as classes of particulars? Extreme versions of realism and nominalism hold that objects are not **substances** but bundles of properties. Bertrand Russell held that objects are bundles of universals; D.C. Williams held that objects are bundles of tropes (unrepeatable **abstract** particulars). Trope theory conceives of properties as particulars: the redness of one billiard ball is distinct from the redness of another exactly resembling billiard ball. Trope theory merits further investigation.

In Chapter 7 we examine one fundamental feature of the world and our experience of it – causation. We make things happen, and natural events produce other events, but what is the nature of the causal relation that underlies these transactions? Hume, respecting his **empiricist** principles, took causation to be a matter of regularity and took the necessity of causation to be a **projection** of the mind upon the world. Hume's theory was criticized by his compatriot and contemporary, Thomas Reid. Hume's regularity theory, along with David Lewis's counterfactual theory, are **reductionist** theories of causation, and both are open to objections. An interesting (non-reductionist) proposal by Elizabeth Anscombe is discussed. At the end of the chapter we defend the coherence of backwards causation.

Chapter 8 is about time. The Cambridge philosopher J.M.E. McTaggart inaugurated the current philosophical debate over the nature of time. McTaggart pointed out that positions in time can be distinguished in two quite different ways. Events can be placed in the B series (and ordered by the earlier-than and later-than relations). They can also be located in the A series (and ordered as past, present or future).

Positions in the B series are permanent; those in the A series are constantly changing. The A theorist embraces the flow of time and holds that the moving *now* is ontologically significant. The B theorist denies that time flows and takes the past and the future to be as real as the present. McTaggart thought he had decisive objections to both theories, and concluded that time is unreal. But McTaggart's objections were not decisive. Which theory is the more plausible? Given the serious problems facing the A theory, the B theory is the clear winner (but not problem-free).

In Chapter 9 we look at three time-related issues. First, we have temporally biased attitudes. We prefer bad experiences to be in the past rather than the future, and we are glad when unpleasant experiences are past rather than present. These attitudes are hard to make sense of on the B theory. Second, Sydney Shoemaker provides an ingenious example of a world in which there is time without change, and in which people in that world can predict when such a change-free period will have elapsed. The possibility of time without change also creates problems for the B theory of time. Finally, we explore the idea of time travel and agree with David Lewis that travel into the past or future is not paradoxical.

In Chapter 10 we are concerned with two sets of challenges to the common sense belief that we have free will. The arguments of the fatalist presuppose that it is either true now that the future will be a particular way or true now that it will not. Whichever way the future turns out, it was fated to turn out thus. Replying to these arguments is a delicate matter, and depends on which theory of time is accepted.

The second challenge to free will stems from the belief that determinism, if true, threatens our free will. The compatibilist holds this threat to be illusory; the libertarian holds it to be real and recommends giving up belief in determinism. Compatibilism and libertarianism are both open to serious objections. Galen Stawson argues that determinism is a red-herring in the free will debate. The real problem is that free will is a logically unsatisfiable, hence incoherent, concept.

In Chapter 11, we are concerned with the nature and existence of facts. Two theories make essential use of facts: the correspondence theory of truth and truthmaker theory. The most famous example of a correspondence theory is the **Logical Atomism** of Wittgenstein's *Tractatus*. Wittgenstein postulates not just the existence of facts, but a structural identity between fact and truth. Truthmaker theory, in contrast, does not require any identity of structure between fact and truth. It holds only that truths have truthmakers, in virtue of which they are true. However, general truths (e.g., all humans are mortal) and negative truths (e.g., there are no unicorns) pose grave problems for truthmaker theory.

In Chapter 12, we look at a range of theories of truth: correspondence and coherence theories, verificationist or anti-realist theories, and deflationary theories. Correspondence, coherence and anti-realist theories all hold that there is a nature to truth: corresponding to the facts, cohering with other beliefs, being in principle knowable, respectively. All three theories face a range of objections. Partly because of these objections, some philosophers have embraced a deflationary view of truth – the view that there is no theoretically interesting nature to truth. On one version of the deflationary view, 'true' is a redundant term: 'it's true that P' says no more than 'P'. But deflationary theories face their own objections too.

• INTERNET RESOURCES

Edward Craig, (1998), 'Metaphysics', *Routledge Encyclopedia of Philosophy*, ed. E. Craig. London: Routledge. Retrieved March 03, 2010, from http://www.rep.routledge.com/article/N095.

Peter van Inwagen, 'Metaphysics', *The Stanford Encyclopedia of Philosophy (Winter 2009 Edition)*, ed. Edward N. Zalta, URL = <http://plato.stanford.edu/archives/win2009/entries/metaphysics/>. http://www.formalontology.com/ontologists.htm.

1

god

• INTRODUCTION

One of the oldest metaphysical questions is: does God exist? In discussing this question, we understand 'God' in the classical philosophical sense of an infinite, **necessary being** who created and sustains the spatio-temporal universe. Such a being is traditionally regarded as all-powerful (**omnipotent**), all-knowing (**omniscient**) and wholly good.

In this chapter, we examine and criticize the three best-known philosophical arguments for God's existence. These are known as the Ontological, Cosmological and Teleological arguments, though there are many versions of each argument.

• THE ONTOLOGICAL ARGUMENT

There have been many different versions of the Ontological Argument throughout the history of philosophy, but the first, and most discussed, is that presented in the 11th century by St Anselm, Archbishop of Canterbury, in his *Proslogion*. Here is a crucial paragraph from which we can reconstruct his argument:

> Thus even the fool is convinced that something than which nothing greater can be conceived is in the understanding, since when he hears this, he understands it; and whatever is understood is in the understanding. And certainly that than which a greater cannot be conceived cannot be in the understanding alone. For if it is ... in the understanding alone, it can be conceived to exist in reality also, which is greater. Thus if that than which a greater cannot be conceived is in the understanding alone, then that than which a greater cannot be conceived is itself that than which a greater can be conceived. But surely this cannot be. Thus without doubt something than which a greater cannot be conceived exists, both in the understanding and reality.[1]

A reconstruction might proceed as follows:

1 God is that than which nothing greater can be conceived.
2 God either exists in the understanding alone or exists both in the understanding and in reality.

3 If God existed in the understanding alone, a greater being could be conceived, namely, a being with all God's qualities who exists both in the understanding and in reality.

4 So God cannot exist in the understanding alone (from 1 and 3).

5 So God exists both in the understanding and in reality (from 2 and 4).

6 So God exists (in reality) (from 5).

Premise (1) is intended to be true by definition. According to Anselm, the word 'God' simply means (among other things) 'that than which no greater can be conceived', just as 'triangle' means 'three-sided plane figure' or 'bachelor' means 'unmarried man'. So the fool could no more sensibly deny that God is that than which nothing greater can be conceived than he could sensibly deny that triangles are three-sided or bachelors unmarried.

Premise (2) is also intended to be truistic, and an instance of the following supposedly quite general truth: for any F that has been conceived, either F exists in the under-standing alone or F exists both in the understanding and in reality. Thus, unicorns and dragons exist in the understanding alone, men and horses exist both in the under-standing and in reality.

Premise (3) is motivated by the following train of thought. Suppose we consider two beings alike in their properties, except only that the first being exists in the under-standing alone, while the second exists both in the understanding and in reality. Then the second being is greater than the first – existence in reality is a great-making property. Given (1), (2) and (3), (6) quickly follows.

ST ANSELM (1033–1109)

Anselm was born in Aosta in Italy. He became a monk and was later appointed Archbishop of Canterbury. As much a theologian as a philosopher, Anselm is credited with putting forward the first version of the Ontological Argument for God's existence. Anselm's belief in God did not rest on his proof; he simply wanted to make manifest God's existence and nature. His Ontological Argument has had a mixed reception: Aquinas and Kant rejected it; Duns Scotus and Descartes proposed their own versions of it. Although the argument has few adherents today, there is no consensus on where the reasoning goes astray.

Criticizing Anselm's proof

How might we criticize Anselm's argument? To start with, we should not assume that all definitions are coherent. Some are not. For example, I might try to define 'meganumber' thus:

(M) Meganumber is that natural number than which there is no larger.

But (M) is incoherent. There is no largest natural number since the natural number series is infinite.

Is there any reason to think that premise (1) is similarly incoherent? There will be if God's great-making qualities are non-maximal (i.e., qualities which can always be possessed to a greater degree, such as height or weight). But, since God is an infinite being, His great-making qualities are maximal. Qualities such as omnipotence, omniscience and perfect goodness are maximal. No being can be more powerful than an omnipotent being, for example. So we cannot criticize Anselm's definition of 'God' as we did definition (M).

It might be objected that, even if premise (1) is coherent, it cannot have any ontological consequences. A mere stipulation cannot generate real entities. When the word 'bachelor' was first introduced into the language and defined as 'unmarried man', the definition alone did not guarantee that the world contained bachelors. Or again, that we have meaningful definitions of words such as 'dragon' and 'unicorn' should not lead anyone to think that such creatures exist. So how can premise (1), a mere definition, possibly have ontological consequences?

However, it would beg the question against Anselm to press this objection at this stage. For Anselm could reasonably reply that, although many definitions have no ontological consequences, his definition does. If we are to criticize Anselm fairly, we must examine the subsequent steps in his reasoning.

Once we do, however, concerns arise immediately. It soon becomes apparent that Anselm has a quite bizarre account of what it is to understand a word. The first three sentences in the quote from Anselm suggest the following chain of thought. I first understand a word 'F' (a **general term**, say, such as 'unicorn' or 'horse'), and thereby grasp the concept of an F. In virtue of possessing the concept, an F exists in my understanding, and has the qualities typical of an F. We can then inquire whether Fs also exist in reality.

Thus, if I understand the word 'unicorn', a unicorn exists in my understanding and has the qualities typically associated with unicorns (four legs, spiral horn, lion's tail, etc.). But this is incredible. When I understand the word 'unicorn', I do not have something four-legged and spiral-horned in my mind! Anselm has committed what we might call the fallacy of reification. He has identified the mind's grasping a concept with the mind's containing the object conceived. But this is to confuse concept with object: the concept is in my mind, but its object is not.

Premises (2) and (3) are glaring examples of the fallacy of reification. Once we recognize that it is a fallacy – that when I understand the word 'God' there is not something in my mind which is omnipotent, omniscient, etc. – we must reject those premises. They are based on an untenable construal of what it is to understand a word.

THE ONTOLOGICAL ARGUMENT

St Anselm's Ontological Argument is a classic example of a rationalist argument. The argument attempts to show that we can establish a substantial conclusion – God's existence – by reason alone. This contradicts the **empiricist** principle (associated with British philosophers such as Locke, Berkeley and Hume) that reason alone can never produce knowledge of reality. The empiricists held that knowledge of reality relies essentially on input from one or more of the five senses. The Ontological Argument is ingenious. It attempts to prove the existence of God merely from the idea or definition of God as 'that than which no greater can be conceived'. It would be extraordinary if a definition of a word could prove the existence of anything beyond itself. Fortunately, it does not.

The parody of Gaunilo the monk

Although the above suffices to dispose of Anselm's version of the Ontological Argument, it's worth mentioning a response made to Anselm by one of his contemporaries, Gaunilo of Marmoutiers. In his 'On Behalf of the Fool', Gaunilo contemplates an island than which no more excellent can be conceived and then writes:

> Now if someone should tell me that there is such an island, I should easily understand his words. ... But suppose he went on to say, as if by a logical inference: 'You can no longer doubt that this island which is more excellent than all islands exists somewhere, since you have no doubt that it is in your understanding. And since it is more excellent not to be in the understanding alone, but to exist both in the understanding and in reality, for this reason it must exist. For if it does not exist, any island which really exists will be more excellent than it; and so the island already understood by you to be more excellent will not be more excellent.[2]

Gaunilo is here attempting a parody of Anselm's proof. That is, he is employing reasoning analogous to Anselm's to establish an obviously absurd conclusion. Clearly the world does not contain a perfect island (that is, an island than which no greater can be conceived), or a perfect car, or a perfect crocodile, etc. If arguments analogous to Anselm's are unsound, Anselm's argument must be unsound too. Note that parody arguments, though potentially effective in one respect, are deficient in another. If successful, a parody argument shows that the original (parodied) argument goes wrong, but it provides no diagnosis of where it goes wrong.

However, as Anselm himself pointed out, Gaunilo's parody fails because his argument is not analogous to Anselm's in a crucial respect. Since God is an infinite being, His great-making qualities are maximal, i.e., qualities which cannot be possessed to a greater degree. But, since islands are finite, the qualities that make an island excellent (abundance of coconuts, white sand, warm sea, etc.) are plainly not maximal. In which case the description 'island than which no greater can be conceived' (like 'natural number than which there is no larger') expresses no coherent concept.

• THE COSMOLOGICAL ARGUMENT

Although rejecting Anselm's Ontological Argument, St Thomas Aquinas (c.1225–1274) advocated the Cosmological Argument for God's existence. This argument can take many forms, one of which is known as the 'Argument from Contingency'. The Jesuit philosopher and historian Frederick Copleston, in a famous debate with Bertrand Russell in 1948, outlined the following version of the Argument from Contingency:

> The series of events [comprising the history of the universe] is either caused, or it is not caused. If it is caused, there must obviously be a cause outside the series. If it is not caused, then it is sufficient to itself; and if it is sufficient to itself it is what I call necessary. But it [the universe] can't be necessary since each member is contingent, and ... the total has no reality apart from its members.[3]

We can reconstruct Copleston's argument as follows:

1 The universe is either contingent or necessary.
2 The universe is not necessary.
3 So, the universe is contingent (from 1 and 2).
4 If contingent, it must have a cause.
5 The cause of the universe must lie outside the universe.
6 Whatever lies outside the universe must be a necessary being.
7 So, there is a necessary being (from 3–6).

The argument is clearly **deductively valid**: if 1–6 are all true, then 7 is true. So the debate will be over the truth of one or more of the premises. Premise 1 I take to be unobjectionable. The universe around us is either contingent (i.e., might not have existed) or necessary (i.e., could not but have existed).

Premise 2 is more controversial. Some philosophers have held that the existence of the universe is necessary. The objects of Wittgenstein's *Tractatus* were held to be necessary objects, the constituents of every possible world. There is a theory of possible worlds – David Lewis's **modal realism** – which holds that our world is one among an infinity of existing **concrete** worlds. Each of Lewis's worlds exists necessarily: our world could not but have been part of the 'pluriverse' of worlds. (See Chapter 4.) But these views are implausible. Intuitively, ours is the only concrete world which exists, and its existence is contingent. It might not have existed. There might have been nothing; no spatio-temporal world at all. In which case, 2 is true.

That our universe is contingent (line 3) is plausible enough in itself, but Copleston attempts to argue for it in a way that may seem to commit the so-called 'fallacy of composition' – the fallacy of assuming that a totality must have a property if each of its elements has that property. Copleston does indeed argue that the spatio-temporal universe is contingent because each of its elements is contingent. Two replies can be made in Copleston's defence:

(i) There is no formal 'fallacy of composition' – it depends on the property in question. As Russell pointed out, it would be fallacious to reason: every human has a mother; so the human race has a mother. But in other cases a totality has a property precisely because each of its elements has that property. A ship is wooden because each of its planks is wooden. Similarly, the universe may be contingent because each of its elements is contingent.

(ii) It's true that Coplestone's reasoning is not logically valid. It could be contingent that A exists, contingent that B exists, contingent that C exists … etc. yet necessary that either A exists or B exists or C exists … etc. But why is the disjunction necessary if each element is contingent? That would require some special explanation.

Let us grant 3 and concentrate on 4–7. Premise 5 is uncontroversial: since no part of a thing can cause itself, the cause of the universe (if there is one) must lie outside the universe. Premise 6 is plausible: anything which lies 'outside' the spatio-temporal universe is presumably a necessary being. More to the point: if the cause of the universe were a contingent being, we could run the 3–7 argument again for that being, and so on. Either we have an infinite regress of contingent beings each the cause of the other or we halt the regress with a necessary being. Copleston assumes that such an infinite regress is impossible since it yields no explanation of the existence of our universe, and so plumps for a necessary being.

ST AQUINAS (c.1225–1274)

Thomas Aquinas was born in Roccasecca in Italy. He studied the works of Aristotle at the University of Naples and then became a Dominican friar. Aquinas's best-known work is his *Summa theologiae* (1266–73). He held that faith and reason cannot conflict, since reason, if properly exercised, will never yield deliverances contrary to faith. Aquinas denied that the existence of God could be proved merely by reflection on the idea of God – hence he rejected Anselm's Ontological Argument. However, he did hold that the existence of God could be established from premises concerning the nature and existence of the universe (*Summa theologiae* 1a, qu. 2, art. 3). These are Aquinas's famous 'five ways' to prove the existence of God, one of which draws on the contingent existence of the universe (a version of the Cosmological Argument).

Questioning premise 4

What then of premise 4? If the universe is contingent, must it have a cause? On the face of it, no. There seem to be three falsifying possibilities:

(i) One might hold, as Aristotle did, that the universe is contingent, yet **eternal**. Since the universe has always existed, it has no cause. It is contingent, but uncaused. Current events have causes stretching back without end. However, the idea of an actual infinite past is difficult to comprehend, though we have no problem with the idea of an endless future. (This may correspond to the difference between actual and potential conceptions of infinity. The latter is easier to grasp.)

Moreover, even if there were an infinite past, the question 'why does our universe exist?' does not thereby vanish. Of course, we cannot ask what caused the universe to exist since it has always existed. But we can still ask: why has our universe always existed? Why this eternal universe rather than nothing? Even here, the theistic answer is still available. Though God could not have caused an eternal universe to exist, He could have sustained it in existence for all time past. There is no incoherence in the idea of one eternal entity depending for its existence on another eternal entity. (Think of an eternal shadow cast by an eternal flame.)

(ii) Some modern cosmologists hold that the universe, though not eternal, had no cause. The existence of the universe was not necessitated (there might not have been any 'Big Bang'), yet it had no cause. The universe is contingent yet uncaused. Centuries earlier, Hume had declared it conceivable that the universe had a beginning but no cause.[4]

There was nothing, then there was something. But the something – the universe – had no cause. Why did the universe pop into existence? No answer can be given. It is difficult to be satisfied with this proposal, and the ancient Greeks were rightly sceptical of it – *Ex nihilo, nihil fit* (Nothing can come from nothing).

(iii) The history of the universe may constitute a massive **causal loop**. Hence, for any two events, A and B, if A causes B, B is part of a chain of events which loops round to cause A. On this scenario, the existence of the universe would be contingent but uncaused. However, this circular dependency scenario encounters the same difficulty as the linear possibilities: we are offered no explanation of how the universe itself came to be.

Summing up

We have four accounts of the nature and origin of our universe: it was created by a necessary being; it has always existed; it had a beginning but no cause; it is circular but uncaused. These accounts appear to exhaust the field – so one of them must be the actual truth about our universe.

A defender of the Cosmological Argument can make a good case for premise 4 by pointing out the difficulties with the non-theistic proposals. I fall short of saying that the Cosmological Argument is fully cogent, but it is surely the most plausible of the standard philosophical arguments for God's existence. However, even if the argument were compelling, its conclusion implies nothing about the moral nature of the necessary being (e.g., whether He is good or loving).

• THE TELEOLOGICAL ARGUMENT

The Teleological Argument for God's existence, also called the Argument from Design, attempts to argue for the existence of God, not from the mere existence of the universe, but from the intricacy and complexity of its structure.

Although the argument has been around since the Stoics, and was defended by Socrates and Aquinas, William Paley (1743–1805) devised the best-known version of it, based on the following analogy. Paley says that when we encounter a stone in a desert, we do not suppose that it had a designer. But if we were to come across a complex instrument, such as a watch, we would assume it had a maker, and we would be justified in this assumption. For by examining its parts, we could see that they were 'framed and put together for a purpose'.[5] Hence we may reasonably conclude that 'the watch must have had a maker. ... There must have been, at some place or other, an artificer or artificers who formed it for the purpose which we find it actually to answer; who comprehended its construction and designed its use.'[6]

Paley then argues that we can reason, in analogous fashion, from the universe we find around us, in particular from complex biological items such as flowers, hearts and eyes, to the existence of a designer of the universe: God. Since we are justified in moving from the existence of a watch to the existence of a watchmaker, we must be equally justified in moving from the existence of complex biological structures to the existence of a creator. Furthermore, the beauty and symmetry of such structures points towards the benevolent nature of their creator.

How should we respond to this argument? Note that, unlike previous arguments, the Teleological Argument is not presented as deductively valid. Since, e.g., some random rearrangement of particles into a watch-like configuration is not impossible, the existence of a watch does not logically guarantee the existence of a watchmaker. Paley's claim is rather that, upon coming across a watch, it is reasonable to believe that it was made by a watchmaker. A watchmaker best explains the existence of the watch. Analogously, on seeing the complex world around us, it is reasonable to believe that it was created by God. God best explains the existence and complexity of the universe.

WILLIAM PALEY (1743–1805)

William Paley studied and taught at the University of Cambridge, before becoming a clergyman in the Church of England. He wrote three major works. In *Principles of Moral and Political Philosophy* (1785) he defended utilitarianism (the view that we ought to do whatever maximizes human happiness) on theological grounds. In *A View of the Evidence of Christianity* (1794) he discussed belief in miracles and commented on the discussion of miracles in Section 10 of Hume's *Enquiry*. *Natural Theology* (1802) is Paley's best-known work, in which he put forward his version of the Teleological Argument, arguing that the complex and varied world around us is best explained as the result of divine creation.

Three objections

(i)   Even if Paley's reasoning were to be found persuasive, the most it would establish is that God created the universe, not that He still exists. Just as we have no reason to think that the watchmaker exists now, so we have no reason to think that God exists now.

(ii) In David Hume's *Dialogues Concerning Natural Religion* (1779), published after Hume's death and before the publication of Paley's 1802 treatise, one of the imaginary participants, Philo, points out how little we are entitled to infer about the creator from observation of the world around us:

> This world, for aught he [a defender of the argument from design] knows, is very faulty and imperfect, compared to a superior standard; and was only the first rude essay of some infant deity, who afterwards abandoned it, ashamed of his lame performance: it is the work only of some dependent, inferior deity; and is the object of derision to his superiors: it is the production of old age and dotage in some superannuated deity; and ever since his death, has run on at adventures, from the first impulse and active force which it received from him.[7]

Relatively few planets are hospitable to life, and even Earth is subject to ice-ages, famines, tsunamis, etc. (not to mention cancer, strokes and heart attacks). Would God not have designed a more congenial environment and biology for his creation?

(iii) Most importantly, we must remember that Paley was writing before Darwin propounded his theory of evolution. For anyone in 1800, the only explanation of the complexity of the universe was divine creation. Paley's reasoning would have seemed then to be the merest common sense. However, from our vantage point, we have another explanation available – Darwin's theory of evolution – and Paley's reasoning no longer seems so inescapable.

If we are wondering how human beings, with all their intricate internal organs (such as eyes and hearts) came to be here, we now have two competing explanations: Darwin's theory of evolution by natural selection and the divine explanation. The theory of evolution has enjoyed great explanatory success, and is so well established that it is not seriously in doubt. It (currently) provides the best explanation for the existence and variety of human and other species. In which case, Paley's reasoning lapses: the eye is not analogous to a found watch. The availability of the Darwinian explanation of the origin of the species has effectively scuppered the Teleological Argument.

The Fine-Tuning Argument

A modern variant of the Teleological Argument – the Fine-Tuning Argument – begins from the observation that had the initial conditions of the universe been slightly different (e.g., had the amount of matter equalled the amount of anti-matter) life would not have evolved. As Derek Parfit puts it:

> For life to be possible, the initial conditions had to be selected with the kind of accuracy that would be needed to hit a bullseye in a distant galaxy. Since it is not arrogant to think life special, this appearance of fine-tuning needs to be explained. Of the countless possible initial conditions, why were the ones that allowed for life also the ones that actually obtained?[8]

Of course, future science may discover that the universe is not as fine-tuned as we had thought. If future science doesn't make such a discovery, three kinds of answer to Parfit's question are possible.

(i)   One answer is theistic: God, whose existence is necessary, arranged things that way.

(ii)   Another answer is that there is no answer. The actual universe just is life-permitting, and no explanation of this can be given. There was a coincidence of initial conditions which allowed the formation of stars and planets, and later allowed life to evolve. But there is no explanation of why just those initial conditions obtained. This response is apt to seem unsatisfying. If the chance of life-permitting initial conditions obtaining is so incredibly low, must there not be an explanation of why those conditions actually obtained?

(iii) There is a third answer:

> Our Universe may not be the whole of reality. Some physicists suggest that there are many other Universes – or, to avoid confusion, worlds. These worlds have the same **laws of nature** as our own world, and they emerged from similar Big Bangs, but each had slightly different initial conditions. On this *many-worlds hypothesis*, there would be no need for fine-tunings. If there were enough Big Bangs, it would be no surprise that, in a few of those, conditions were just right for life. And it would be no surprise that our Big Bang was one of those few.[9]

In other words, if our world is merely one among many life-permitting worlds, it is not so mysterious that our world is life-permitting: many worlds are, and ours happens to be one of them. Certain interpretations of quantum mechanics, and the doctrine of modal realism (see Chapter 4), would endorse this third answer.

• CONCLUDING REMARKS

The three standard arguments for God's existence are all open to objections. However, the Cosmological Argument shows the most promise, and may even be a cogent proof of God's existence. There is also a cunning modal version of the Ontological Argument, discussed in Chapter 4.

• STUDY QUESTIONS

- How would you defend Anselm's Ontological Argument?
- What does Gaunilo's parody show?
- Does our universe exist of necessity?
- Can something come from nothing?
- How plausible is the Fine-Tuning Argument? Does it represent any advance over the standard Teleological Argument?

• ANNOTATED FURTHER READING

J.L. Mackie, *The Miracle of Theism* (Oxford: Clarendon Press, 1982). An excellent introduction to all the major arguments for and against God's existence. Highly recommended.

A. Plantinga (ed.), *The Ontological Argument* (New York: Anchor Books, 1965). A useful little book, in two parts. In the first part, Plantinga selects presentations of the Ontological Argument from Anselm, Descartes, Spinoza and Leibniz, alongside various critical commentaries. Plantinga selects a (now rather dated but still interesting) collection of 20th-century commentators.

A. Plantinga, *God, Freedom and Evil* (London: Allen & Unwin, 1975). In this useful book Plantinga outlines and criticizes the standard arguments for God's existence, and ends by defending a version of the Ontological Argument.

W.L. Rowe, *The Cosmological Argument* (Princeton, NJ: Princeton University Press, 1975). A very clear, detailed and historically informed discussion of all aspects of the Cosmological Argument.

• INTERNET RESOURCES

A. Plantinga (1998), 'God, Arguments for the Existence of', *Routledge Encyclopedia of Philosophy*, ed. E. Craig. Retrieved 31 May 2006 from <http://www.rep.routledge. com/ article/K029>.

G. Oppy, 'Ontological Arguments', *The Stanford Encyclopedia of Philosophy* (Fall 2005 edition), ed. Edward N. Zalta. Retrieved 31 May 2006 from <http://plato. stanford. edu/archives/fall2005/entries/ontological-arguments>.

Del Ratzsch, 'Teleological Arguments for God's Existence', *The Stanford Encyclopedia of Philosophy* (Winter 2009 Edition), ed. Edward N. Zalta, URL = <http:// plato.stanford.edu/archives/win2009/entries/teleological-arguments/>.

Bruce Reichenbach, 'Cosmological Argument', *The Stanford Encyclopedia of Philosophy* (Spring 2010 Edition), ed. Edward N. Zalta, forthcoming, URL = <http://plato. stanford.edu/archives/spr2010/entries/cosmological-argument/>.

• NOTES

1. Anselm Proslogion II in *St Anselm's Proslogion*, ed. M. Charlesworth (Oxford: Oxford University Press, 1965), p.116.
2. Gaunilo, 'On Behalf of the Fool', in *St Anselm's Proslogion*, pp. 163–5
3. 'Must God Exist?', in *Philosophy in the Open* (Milton Keynes: Open University Press, 1978), pp. 119–120.
4. D. Hume, *A Treatise of Human Nature*, Book 1, Part III, Sec 3.
5. W. Paley, *Natural Theology*, ed. F. Ferre (New York: Bobbs-Merrill Co. Inc., 1963), pp. 1–2.
6. *Ibid.*, p. 2.
7. D. Hume, *Dialogues Concerning Natural Religion*, ed. N. Kemp Smith, 2nd edn (London: Nelson, 1947), p. 168.
8. D. Parfit, 'The Puzzle of Reality: Why Does the Universe Exist?', *Times Literary Supplement* (3 July 1992), pp. 3–5.
9. *Ibid.*, pp. 3–5.

2

what are we?

• INTRODUCTION

One of the most fundamental question in metaphysics is: what are we? Of course, we are lots of things: e.g., butchers, bakers and candlestick makers. But what are we fundamentally? This question is of intrinsic interest to us. It has implications for our survival after death, and for our conception of how we interact with the world. In this chapter, we will look at a number of theories of what we are, and hence of what it is for us to continue to exist.

• WHAT ARE WE?

Here are four theories of what we fundamentally are:

(i)   *Dualism*: we are immaterial souls.

(ii) *Animalism*: we are human beings.

(iii) *Constitutionalism*: we are constituted by, but not identical with, human beings.

(iv) *Humeanism*: we are 'bundles of perceptions'.

On the first two views, we are **substances**. That is, we are unified, self-contained subjects of experience, whose nature and unity are conceptually – if not causally – independent of other entities. Contrast, e.g., smiles or scratches, which are conceptually dependent on people and surfaces, respectively. To think of a scratch is to think of it as a scratch of some surface. The Dualist holds that we are immaterial substances, persisting through time but lacking spatial characteristics. The Animalist holds that we are biological substances in space and time.

According to Constitutionalism and Humeanism, we are not substances. On the Constitutionalist view, we are unified but dependent entities constituted out of genuine substances, human beings. On Hume's view, we lack any substantial principle of unity. We are mere bundles or collections of mental states, causally dependent on human brains and bodies.

Notice that I have not included the following answer:

(v)   We are persons.

I exclude this answer since it does not tell us what we fundamentally are. It merely postpones the answer to that question. Locke famously defined a person as 'a thinking, intelligent being, that has reason and reflection, and can consider itself as itself, the same thinking thing, in different times and places'.[1] A person is a self-conscious, reflective being, capable of engaging in a range of first-person thoughts ('I will take luncheon at Tetsuya's today', 'I might have dined at Le Normandie in Bangkok last night', etc.). This is a perfectly reasonable definition of 'person', which rightly classifies most of us as persons most of the time, but it signally fails to tell us what we are. It does not help us decide between theories (i) – (iv).

We can make some preliminary comments about our four candidate theories.

Dualism

Rene Descartes held that we are a union of non-physical or immaterial soul and physical body. In his *Sixth Meditation* Descartes wrote that 'I have a clear and distinct idea of myself, in so far as I am a thinking, non-extended thing; and ... I have a clear and distinct idea of body, in so far as this is simply an extended, non-thinking thing. ... [A]ccordingly it is certain that I am really distinct from my body, and can exist without it.'[2]

The soul only has mental properties, the body only has physical ones. Soul and body are distinct substances – the soul essentially a non-extended thinking substance, the body essentially an extended non-thinking substance – and the soul can survive the death of the body. The soul is a simple or indivisible mental substance, whose identity over time is primitive and unanalysable.

THOMAS REID (1710–1796)

Thomas Reid was born and educated in Aberdeen, Scotland. He taught at King's College, Aberdeen, until he succeeded Adam Smith to the Chair of Moral Philosophy at Glasgow University in 1764. He resigned from that Chair in 1781 in order to write more, and subsequently published *Essays on the Intellectual Powers of Man* (1785) (a development of his earlier (1764) *Inquiry into the Human Mind on the Principles of Common Sense*) and *Essays on the Active Powers of Man* (1788). Reid inaugurated the school of 'Scottish Common Sense Philosophy' and held that the mind was innately capable of forming a number of principles of common sense which, though not susceptible of proof, were the foundation for all cognitive activity. Reid was critical of Hume: the mind is active not passive; we directly perceive external objects not mental items; the self is an indivisible substance not a bundle of perceptions; regularities do not amount to causation; the only real causation is agent causation (which also accounts for our free will). Reid was also critical of Locke's claim that memory constitutes personal identity. Memories yield direct knowledge of one's past, but do not make for sameness of person.

Thomas Reid and Joseph Butler (1692–1752) both endorsed the Dualist view of ourselves. Reid talked of the 'continued existence of that indivisible thing which I call myself. Whatever this self may be, it is something which thinks, and deliberates and resolves, and acts, and suffers. I am not thought, I am not action, I am not feeling; I am something that thinks, and acts, and suffers.'[3]

As a consequence of this Reid wrote that identity:

> has no fixed nature when applied to bodies and very often questions about it are questions about words. But identity when applied to persons has no ambiguity and admits not of degrees or of more or less. It is the foundation of all rights and obligations and of all account-ableness, and the notion of it is fixed and precise.[4]

Similarly, Butler held that the word 'same' is used in a 'strict and philosophical sense' when applied to persons, but in a 'loose and popular' sense when applied to bodies and other kinds of thing (e.g., artefacts).

Thus, whereas it may be a verbal question whether to call this, much altered, car the 'same car' as the Jaguar I bought ten years ago, it is never a verbal question whether I or others continue to exist. Our identity over time cannot be settled by stipulation.

Animalism

What of the Animalists' answer? Here is an early statement of Animalism by David Wiggins:

> Perhaps x is a person **if and only if** x is an animal falling under the extension of a kind whose typical members perceive, feel, remember, imagine, desire, acquire a character as they age, are happy or miserable, are susceptible to concern for members of their own or like species ... have, and conceive of themselves as having, a past accessible in experience-memory and a future accessible in intention ... etc.[5]

Wiggins is doing two things here: (i) he is attempting to characterise or elucidate our concept of a person; (ii) he is claiming that the concept *person* is a restriction or qualification of the concept *animal*, thus implying that necessarily all persons are animals.

Later Animalists (such as Eric Olson) reject both (i) and (ii). Animalism is not seen as offering any new definition or elucidation of what it is to be a person. Locke's definition did that adequately enough. Nor is Animalism claiming that necessarily all persons are animals. On the contrary, Animalism is consistent with the possibility of soul-persons or robot-persons.

The distinctive thesis of contemporary Animalism is that we terrestials are human beings. The pronoun 'I' in each of our mouths refers to a human being. In other words, for any human person x, x is numerically identical to the human being in x's shoes. This is the central thesis of Animalism as I will understand it here.

Nonetheless, Animalism as I understand it does share the following crucial thesis in common with Wiggins' account: the concept *person* is not the concept of a fundamental kind of thing. It is always a restriction of a more fundamental concept. Thus human persons are fundamentally human beings; in robot worlds, robot-persons are fundamentally robots; in soul worlds, soul-persons are fundamentally souls.

A real-life example illustrates this point. A human being can survive in a coma, irretrievably devoid of mentality. According to Animalism, if this fate befell me, I would continue to exist, though no person would then occupy my body. So I can exist without being a person. Hence *person* is not the concept of a fundamental kind of thing. We are fundamentally human beings (animals of a certain sort) and only **contingently** do we fall under the concept *person*.

ANIMALISM

Animalism is not the implausible view that, of necessity, all persons are animals. This is implausible since we can conceive of worlds in which persons are, e.g., silicon-based lifeforms. Animalism's central claim is that we terrestials are fundamentally animals (in our case, human beings) and not fundamentally self-reflective, self-conscious beings (i.e., persons). You are identical to the human animal in your shoes, and your conditions of identity over time are those of a human being. Despite its intuitive and no-nonsense character, Animalism cannot be correct. There are clearly conceivable scenarios in which I survive, but the animal in my shoes does not. In which case, I cannot be identical to that animal.

Constitutionalism

This view occupies a kind of half-way house between Dualism and Animalism. According to Constitutionalism, we are not immaterial souls, but nor are we numerically identical to any material or biological substance (such as a brain, body or human being). We are, however, constituted by such a substance.

A simple model for Constitutionalism is provided by the relation between a lump and the statue it constitutes. (See Chapter 5.) Thus suppose that a lump of gold, L, is fashioned into a statue, S. Since L existed before S, L ≠ S. Even so, there is no temptation to regard S as a ghostly, immaterial entity. L constitutes S without remainder, and S has all L's physical properties. Or consider the collection of planks from which I build my boat. A few years later I dismantle the boat and use the planks to build a hut. Since the boat is not identical to the hut, the collection of planks cannot be identical first to the boat and then to the hut. Yet that collection constitutes first the boat then the hut. Similarly, according to the Constitutionalist, we are constituted without remainder by a biological substance (a human being), yet numerically distinct from that substance.

The motivation for Constitutionalism is based on (i) an unwillingness to embrace Dualism; and (ii) the belief that some possibilities for me are not possibilities for the human being that constitutes me, and vice versa, and hence I cannot be numerically identical to (one and the same as) a human being.

Humeanism

David Hume thought that persons were not substances, but bundles of perceptions. A bundle or collection has no substantial principle of unity. If experiences e1 and e2 belong to a single person that is not because they **inhere** in the same substance (whether biological or psychic). In elucidation of the bundle view, Hume compared 'the soul ... to a republic or commonwealth, in which the several members are united by the reciprocal ties of government and subordination, and give rise to other persons, who propagate the same republic in the incessant changes of its parts'.[6]

A modern Humean, Derek Parfit, has made much of this analogy. Just as the constituents of a republic (its inhabitants and land) can be understood without reference to the concept of a republic, so the constituents of the self (thoughts, experiences, brains, bodies, etc.) can be understood without reference to the concept of a person. Hume's analogy provides the model for Parfit's **reductionism** about persons.

The Humean view is often characterized as a kind of reductionism, since it attempts to reduce the self to its constituent parts. Parfit's version – the Impersonality thesis – is explicitly reductionist. According to the Impersonality thesis:

1 The fact of a person's identity over time just consists in the holding of certain more particular facts.
2 These facts can be described without either presupposing the identity of this person, or explicitly claiming that the experiences in this person's life are had by this person, or even explicitly claiming that this person exists. These facts can be described in an impersonal way.
3 Though persons exist, we could give a complete description of reality without claiming that persons exist.[7]

Parfit's idea is that a description of reality can be (i) complete, i.e., account for all truths, and (ii) impersonal, i.e., make no reference (explicit or implicit) to persons or subjects of experience. In particular, the mental features that make up our psychological lives (pains, tickles, beliefs, desires, intentions, memories, etc.) can be completely described without reference to a subject who has or owns such mental characteristics, much as the bricks of a house can be completely described without reference to the house that they compose.

• ADJUDICATING THE RIVAL VIEWS

Against Animalism

Let's begin by looking at a set of compelling objections to Animalism. According to the Animalist, we are each identical to the human being in our shoes. So if 'A' names the human being in my shoes, I = A. Now, in general, if X = Y then, by the logic of **numerical identity**, every property of X is a property of Y, and vice versa. This means that if I = A then every possibility for me must be a possibility for A, and vice versa. But there seem to be a range of metaphysically possible scenarios in which either A survives but I do not or in which I survive but A does not. In which case it cannot be true that (here and now) I = A. Here are five such scenarios.

(i)   The coma case described above has been thought by some to tell against Animalism. Some would say that, in such a case, A survives but – since A is irretrievably devoid of mental life – I do not survive.

(ii) Consider the following **thought-experiment**, first introduced into the literature by Sydney Shoemaker:

> It is now possible to transplant certain organs. ... It is at least conceivable ... that a human body could continue to function normally if its brain were replaced by one taken from another human body. ... Two men, a Mr Brown and a Mr Robinson, had been operated on for brain tumours, and brain extractions had been performed on both of them. At the end of the operations, however, the assistant inadvertently put Brown's brain in Robinson's head, and Robinson's brain in Brown's head. One of these men immediately dies, but the other, the one with Robinson's head and Brown's brain, eventually regains consciousness. Let us call the latter 'Brownson'. ... When asked his name he automatically replies 'Brown'. He recognizes Brown's wife and family. ... And is able to describe in detail events in Brown's life ... of Robinson's life he evidences no knowledge at all.[8]

Almost everyone agrees that the best description of this case is that Brown is Brownson. Few think: Brown dies and Robinson acquires a new brain and psychology. So if I underwent such an operation, I would survive in a new body, but A would cease to exist. It's true that part of A (his brain) would continue to exist, but A would no longer exist.

(iii) Suppose that my consciousness-supporting cerebrum is removed from my skull and the rest of my body destroyed. My cerebrum is placed in a vat and kept alive by a machine. I am conscious throughout. Plausibly, I have survived, albeit in a vastly denuded condition. But no animal has survived; A was destroyed.

(iv) We can imagine that technology has reached such an advanced stage that all biological organs, including the brain, can be replaced with bionic organs which serve the very same functions as the animal originals, including psychological functioning. So we could imagine that I go through a process of total bionic replacement. Every part of me is (gradually) replaced with a bionic part. At the end of the process no animal part, hence no animal, remains. Provided the replacement process in no way interferes with my psychology, abilities and appearance (which assumes that my mental states can be realized in a bionic brain), it is very plausible to say that I survive. Yet no animal has survived.

(v)   As a highly trained athlete and thinker, I am naturally invited to be part of the first manned mission to Mars. The mission is a success and after a few months on Mars we return to Earth. After a routine check-up, doctors discover, despite no change to my appearance or mental life, that all my biological matter has been transformed into a hitherto unknown silicon-based life-form. There is no animal (human or otherwise) in my shoes anymore! Hence, A no longer exists. But I continue to exist. (Note that, in so describing cases (iv) and (v), I assume the plausible principle that if x is (identical to) an animal, then x is essentially an animal. So A could not become a non-animal.)

In (i) some think I do not survive while A continues to exist. In (ii) – (v) it is very plausible to judge that I survive while A does not. Given the *prima facie* plausibility of these judgements, it is reasonable to conclude that Animalism must be wrong.

Against Constitutionalism

The Constitutionalist holds, on the basis of the anti-Animalist thought-experiments, that I ≠ A. Now I am a self-conscious subject of experience, a person. But what about the human being, A, in my shoes. Is he self-conscious? There are only two possible answers.

Suppose the Constitutionalist says: 'No: A is just an animal and so has no mental states only physical ones.' The trouble with this answer is that A has all my physical attributes, including my brain and brain states. It is now generally accepted, and accepted by the Constitutionalist, that mental states are causally dependent on brain states. But then why deny the full range of mental states to A? 'No' cannot be the right answer.

Suppose the Constitutionalist says 'Yes, fair enough, A has all Garrett's mental states and is self-conscious.' But remember that the question we're answering arose on the assumption that I ≠ A. So if I am self-conscious, and it is now conceded that A is self-conscious too, it follows that there are two people in my shoes! Generalizing from my case, it follows that the population of the planet is twice what we thought it was. But this is absurd. 'Yes' cannot be the right answer either.

The dilemma is fatal for the Constitutionalist. It shows that the defining tenets of Constitutionalism – (i) we are not identical to human beings, (ii) we are unified subjects of mental states, and (iii) we are not immaterial souls – are mutually inconsistent.

DEREK PARFIT (1942 TO PRESENT)

Educated at Eton and Balliol College, Oxford, Parfit was elected a Prize Fellow at All Souls College, Oxford in 1967. He has remained there ever since, but regularly visits Harvard and New York universities. Parfit has published a number of landmark papers, beginning with 'Personal Identity' (1971), but his most significant work to date is his book *Reasons and Persons* (1984). Much of this rich and ingenious work is devoted to undermining the self-interest theory of rationality. Parfit offers many arguments against this theory, including arguments based on his theory of personal identity. If, as he claims, identity is not what matters, then the self-interest theory loses all force. In the final part of his book, Parfit discusses puzzles and paradoxes arising from our ability to affect both the identity and quality of life of future generations. We need a new theory of beneficence in order to give a satisfactory account of these matters, but Parfit admits that he has not yet found such a theory. His new book *On What Matters* is forthcoming (as of 2010) with Oxford University Press.

Against Humeanism

According to the Humean view, persons are not mental substances or unified subjects of experience. Parfit's Impersonality thesis – that we can give a complete description of reality without mentioning persons – captures one main idea behind the Humean view. Consider the following statements:

1 there exists a particular brain and body, and a particular series of interrelated mental and physical events;

and

2 there exists a particular person.

According to Parfit, a complete and impersonal description of reality is possible provided the following two conditions hold:

(i) (1) can be fully understood without reference to persons.

(ii) (1) and (2) either describe the same fact or (1) entails (2).

But both conditions are open to serious doubt. Condition (i) faces the following two problems. First, it is hard to make sense of simple mental states, such as pains and tickles, other than as had by a subject or person. We can make little sense of an unowned or free-floating tickle. Second, a special problem is posed by more sophisticated mental states such as memory and intention. These states seem to have reference to persons built into their content. My memory of tasting coffee yesterday not only requires a current bearer but appears to implicate me in its content: I remember that

I tasted coffee yesterday. How then can memory, a crucial feature of our psychological lives, be described impersonally?

Parfit's reply is that memory is a composite concept built up out of identity and quasi-memory (q-memory). The latter concept is stipulated to be like memory in all phenomenological and causal respects, yet does not presuppose identity. Thus, e.g. as a result of a donor brain graft, I can have q-memories of someone else's experiences. What we call memories are just q-memories of our own experiences. Q-memories thus yield knowledge of one's own, or another's, past. The crucial, and currently unresolved, question is whether memory is a composite concept or whether it is a unitary concept not reducible to more basic conceptual atoms.[9]

Condition (ii) is also open to question. To start with, if (1) and (2) described the same fact, then there would be no reason to regard (2) as reducible to (1) rather than vice versa. Moreover, (1) and (2) describe the same fact only if a person is identical to his brain and body – a claim at odds with the most plausible description of the anti-Animalist thought-experiments discussed above.

What of the weaker condition that (1) entail (2)? Even if (1) entails (2), we will have reason to regard (1), rather than (2), as the reductionist base only if (2) does not entail (1). So let us take Parfit's proposal to be that (1) entails (2) while (2) does not entail (1). If (1) entails (2), then necessarily if my brain, body, etc. exist, I exist (in that same body). If (2) fails to entail (1), then I could have had a different brain, body, etc.

This combination of views is not contradictory, but it is odd. Call my (living) brain and body A. If (2) fails to entail (1), then there is a possible world in which I occupy a completely different brain and body, B. If (1) entails (2), then in every world in which A exists, I occupy A. This means that there is no world in which A and B both exist and I occupy B. But if it is possible for me to occupy B, and B and A are completely distinct, non-overlapping, entities, why is it be impossible for me to occupy B in a world in which A also exists?

Dualism?

Animalism, Constitutionalism and Humeanism all face serious problems. What then of Dualism? One standard worry concerns the possibility of causal interaction between the immaterial or non-physical soul (which is the bearer of immaterial mental states) and the physical world. For interact they plainly do: stick a pin in your leg and you cause a sensation of pain; given a belief about the whereabouts of the coffee and a desire for coffee, coffee-making behaviour will typically ensue.

This is not an insuperable problem. None of the theories of causation we examine in Chapter 7 – the regularity theory, the counterfactual theory and the derivation theory – exclude the possibility of physical/non-physical causation. It's true that Hume himself would have disallowed physical/non-physical causation since he insists that cause and effect must be contiguous in space. But the regularity theory, as stated in Chapter 7, does not have this stipulation.

Even so, the interactionist Dualist faces another problem. We have good reason to think that the physical world is causally closed, i.e., that physical effects have physical causes, sufficient to explain their effects. The success of science (e.g., explaining lightning in terms of electrical discharge or plant growth in terms of cell division) makes it reasonable to believe that the physical is causally closed.

The Dualist maintains that mental states are non-physical and cause (physical) behaviour. Hence, the Dualist must hold that some physical events (e.g., my hand rising) have non-physical causes (e.g., my desire to acknowledge a friend).

Interactionist Dualism is not incompatible with the causal closure of the physical. But compatibility is secured at the cost of commitment to an implausible **over-determination** thesis. The Dualist would be committed to the claim that human actions have two separate causes, one physical and one non-physical, each sufficient to bring about their effect. Though events are sometimes over-determined, it is hard to believe that every human action involves such over-determination.

The Dualist is caught in an uncomfortable dilemma: deny the causal closure of the physical or commit to a counter-intuitive over-determination. The Dualist could deny the causal efficacy of the mental (i.e., become an **epiphenomenalist** rather than interactionist Dualist), but that is hardly a congenial position either.

DUALISM

For millennia Dualism was the received view of our nature. We were said to be possessed of a physical body and a non-physical (possibly immortal) soul. The soul was held to be a unified mental substance, the true bearer of our mental characteristics, and capable of existence independently of the body. In the 20th century many philosophers were converted to a materialist view of ourselves and our minds. But contemporary popularity is no guarantee of truth, and the Dualist view of ourselves deserves to be taken seriously.

Considerations in favour of Dualism

On the Dualist view, we are immaterial souls whose identity over time is primitive and unanalysable. As a consequence, our identity over time is 'fixed and precise' (to quote Reid), admitting not of degree, ambiguity or indeterminacy. Dualism thus contradicts one of the central claims of Parfit's ingenious 1971 article 'Personal Identity'.[10]

In that article Parfit questioned our natural belief that our identity over time is always an all-or-nothing matter. According to this natural belief, either I will exist in some future situation or I won't; there can be no grey area. Parfit points out that we don't think this in the case of nations or machines. We don't think there has to be a **'yes or**

no' answer to 'Was England the same nation after 1066?' Nor, says Parfit, should we think this with regard to our identity over time.

The Dualist disagrees. Any future situation either contains me or fails to contain me. There can be no indeterminacy in our identity over time. Intuition is, I think, on the side of the Dualist. We can make sense of indeterminacy in the identity of artefacts such as ships. Suppose I quickly remove and replace half the planks making up my ship. Is the resulting ship identical to the earlier one? This question may indeed receive no straightforward answer. It is indeterminate whether the earlier ship is the later one. But it is much harder to make sense of such indeterminacy in the case of persons, especially when we consider the matter from the first-person point of view. Bernard Williams was the first to press this point in his illuminating article 'The Self and the Future'.[11]

Williams points out that we have no model for anticipating, or emotionally responding to, indeterminacy in our own case. He writes:

> To be told that a future situation is a borderline one for its being myself that is hurt, that it is conceptually undecidable whether it will be me or not, is something which, it seems, I can do nothing with; because, in particular, it seems to have no comprehensible representation in my expectations and the emotions that go with them.[12]

An indeterminate or conceptually undecidable case is not like one where I am told that one of us in the room will be shot tomorrow. In that case, I know what the two possibilities are: either I will be the one shot or I won't. Nor is it like the case where I think that some 'nameless horror' will befall me. Either the horror will befall me or it won't. But if I am told that someone tomorrow will suffer great pain, and then told that it is indeterminate whether I am that person, I have no idea how to react. No cognitive or emotional response fits this case. There is, as Williams says, 'an obstinate bafflement to mirroring in my expectations a situation in which it is conceptually undecidable whether I occur'.[13]

It is a point in favour of Dualism that it disallows the possibility of indeterminacy in our identity over time, and a point against theories that allow such indeterminacy (which is most of the contemporary theories of our nature and identity).

• CONCLUDING REMARKS

In this chapter I have outlined and criticized a range of theories concerning our nature and identity. Animalism, Constitutionalism and Humeanism were all found to have serious defects. This left Dualism which, though neither popular nor free of difficulty, offers a natural and intuitive conception of what we are.

• STUDY QUESTIONS

- Are we fundamentally mental beings?
- What is it to think of ourselves as substances?

- Do thought-experiments such as Brain Transplant refute Animalism?
- What is Hume's view of the self?
- Should we be Dualists?

• ANNOTATED FURTHER READING

B. Garrett, *Personal Identity and Self-Consciousness* (London: Routledge, 1998). A hard-to-put-down romp through personal identity and related issues.

H. Noonan, *Personal Identity* (London: Routledge, 2003), 2nd edn. An excellent, if demanding, introduction to the history of the topic and to the contemporary debate.

E. Olson, *The Human Animal* (New York: Oxford University Press, 1997), A clear defence of Animalism.

D. Parfit, *Reasons and Persons* (Oxford: Oxford University Press, 1984), Part III. This book has largely set the agenda for recent discussions of personal identity. Although not introductory, Parfit writes clearly and any interested reader should be able to follow Parfit's radical and revisionary train of thought.

L. Rudder Baker, *Persons and Bodies: A Constitution View* (Cambridge: Cambridge University Press, 2000). A comprehensive defence of Constitutionalism.

S. Shoemaker and R. Swinburne, *Personal Identity* (Oxford: Basil Blackwell, 1984). A very readable debate between a leading defender of the Dualist view (Swinburne) and a leading opponent of that view (Shoemaker).

D. Wiggins, *Sameness and Substance Renewed* (Cambridge: Cambridge University Press, 2001). One of the most important works of metaphysics in the last 50 years. In the final chapter Wiggins defends a version of Animalism and criticizes Parfit's use of the notion of q-memory.

• INTERNET RESOURCES

Rebecca Copenhaver, 'Reid on Memory and Personal Identity', *The Stanford Encyclopedia of Philosophy* (Spring 2009 Edition), ed. Edward N. Zalta, URL = <http://plato.stanford.edu/archives/spr2009/entries/reid-memory-identity/>.

B. Garrett (1998, 2004), 'Personal Identity', *Routledge Encyclopedia of Philosophy*, ed. E. Craig. Retrieved 31 May 2006 from <http://www.rep.routledge.com/article/V024>.

E.T. Olson (2002), 'Personal Identity', *The Stanford Encyclopedia of Philosophy* (Fall 2002 edition), ed. Edward N. Zalta. Retrieved 31 May 2006 from <http://plato.stanford.edu/archives/fall2002/entries/identity-personal>.

Howard Robinson, 'Dualism', *The Stanford Encyclopedia of Philosophy* (Fall 2009 Edition), ed. Edward N. Zalta, URL = <http://plato.stanford.edu/archives/fall2009/entries/dualism/>.

• NOTES

1.   J. Locke, *Essay Concerning Human Understanding*, ed. W. Carroll (Bristol: Thoemmes, 1990), II, xxvii, 9.
2.   R. Descartes, *Meditations on First Philosophy*, ed. J. Cottingham (Cambridge, Cambridge University Press, 1996), p. 54.
3.   T. Reid, *Essays on the Intellectual Powers of Man*, ed. A. Woozley (London: Macmillan, 1941), 3.4, p. 264.
4.   *Ibid.*, p. 16
5.   D. Wiggins, *Sameness and Substance* (Oxford: Blackwell, 1980), p. 171. Note that this definition does not appear in the 2001 edition.
6.   David Hume, *A Treatise of Human Nature* (1739), Book 1, Part IV, Section VI, paragraph 19.
7.   D. Parfit, *Reasons and Persons* (London: Oxford University Press, 1984), pp. 210–12. My (1), (2) and (3) are his (1), (2) and (9).
8.   S. Shoemaker, *Self-Knowledge and Self-Identity* (Ithaca, NY: Cornell University Press, 1963), pp. 23–4.
9.   For doubts about the notion of q-memory, and whether it can serve Parfit's purposes, see D. Wiggins *Sameness and Substance Renewed* (Cambridge: Cambridge University Press, 2001), pp. 214–25 and J.H. McDowell 'Reductionism and the First Person', in *Reading Parfit*, ed. J. Dancy (Oxford: Basil Blackwell, 1997).
10.   D. Parfit, 'Personal Identity', *Philosophical Review*, 80 (1971), pp. 3–27. See also his discussion with Godfrey Vesey, 'Brain Transplants and Personal Identity', in *Philosophy in the Open* (Milton Keynes: Open University Press, 1978).
11.   B. Williams, 'The Self and the Future', in his collection *Problems of the Self* (Cambridge: Cambridge University Press, 1982), pp. 46–64, especially pp. 58–63.
12.   *Ibid.*, p. 58.
13.   *Ibid.*, p. 61

3
existence

- **INTRODUCTION**

Existence gives rise to a host of distinctively philosophical questions that lie at the heart of metaphysics. We need to distinguish the question 'What exists?' from the question 'What is existence?'. Much of metaphysics is concerned with answering questions in the former category: does God exist?; do souls exist?; do past and future objects exist?; do merely possible objects exist?; do numbers exist?; do facts exist? and so on. These questions are addressed in various chapters throughout this book.

But this chapter is concerned with the other question: what is existence? What is it for something to exist? Although this is a question in metaphysics, it is intimately bound up with questions in philosophical logic, questions concerning meaning, reference and logical structure. In answering the 'what is existence?' question, we will have occasion to consider the view that there are objects which do not exist (non-existent objects).

BERTRAND RUSSELL (1872–1970)

Bertrand Russell was born in Monmouthshire, England, of an aristocratic family (he inherited the titles of Earl and Viscount later in life). Both his parents died while he was an infant and he was raised by his strongly religious grandparents. He studied at Trinity College, Cambridge, where, under McTaggart's influence, he was (briefly) an idealist. He later taught at Trinity as a contemporary of G.E. Moore, counting Wittgenstein among his pupils. Russell wrote extensively in almost every branch of philosophy, most significantly in logic, philosophy of mathematics, philosophy of language and mind, and epistemology, but also in social and political philosophy. The latter writings were intended for a general audience. A great prose stylist, he was awarded the Nobel Prize for Literature in 1950. Two of his books – *The Problems of Philosophy* (1912) and *A History of Western Philosophy* (1945) – were philosophical bestsellers. Among his most important and influential philosophical contributions were the Theory of Descriptions and what is known as 'Russell's paradox' (which showed that the intuitive 'axiom of comprehension' – to each property there corresponds a set of exactly the objects with that property – leads to paradox).

• WHAT IS EXISTENCE?

This question is not to be answered by staring at one's navel, inhaling mind-altering substances, or reading the works of Martin Heidegger. In asking 'What is existence?' our aim is to uncover the nature (if any) of existence, but our method will be logico-linguistic. We begin with some typical sentences we utter using the grammatical predicate 'exists' and its negative counterpart 'not exist'. We can divide these into positive and negative existential claims, which then divide into singular and plural predications. So, for example, we have 'Obama exists' (positive singular) and 'tigers exist' (positive plural), and we have 'Santa Claus does not exist' (negative singular) and 'unicorns do not exist' (negative plural). The philosophical problems arise in accounting for the truth of such true existential claims.

If a sentence is true, it is natural to think that there is something that makes it true, something in virtue of which it is true. This intuition holds for true existential sentences as much as for any other true sentence. But in order to be clear about the nature of the truthmaker for (true) existential sentences, we need to be clear about the logical structure of existential sentences.

In the case of an ordinary sentence, such as 'Fred is fat', many contemporary philosophers are happy to regard its grammatical structure as a guide to its logical structure: *viz.*, subject–predicate (i.e., of the form 'Fa', where 'a' is the subject term and 'F' the predicate). The sentence predicates a property (fatness) of a subject (Fred), and it's true just if the subject has the property in question. This naive analysis of sentences like 'Fred is fat' has been called into question (e.g., by Russell, who thought ordinary proper names were not genuine referring expressions), but it is a natural starting point. However, for existential sentences there is controversy over the very starting point.

Let us begin with the simplest case: a true positive singular existential sentence, such as 'Obama exists'. Grammatically, this is a subject–predicate sentence. That is not in dispute. The dispute concerns whether its logical structure is its grammatical structure. There are two opposing views: the property view and the quantifier view.

The property view

The property view holds that the surface grammar is the real grammar. The logical form of 'Obama exists' is as it appears: subject–predicate. 'Obama' refers to Barack Obama, the 44th US President; the predicate 'exists' refers to the property of existence. Just as Fred has the property of fatness, so Obama has the property of existence. On this view, existence is a property of people and other objects, on a par with ordinary properties such as weight, height, baldness, etc.

The quantifier view

On the quantifier view, surface grammar and logical grammar come apart. There are uncontroversial cases of this elsewhere in language. Consider, for example:

(1) The average family has 2.3 children.

This sentence is grammatically subject–predicate. Yet the subject term 'the average family' is a dummy **singular term**, and the predicate 'has 2.3 childen' is a dummy predicate. The function of 'the average family' is not to refer to some particular family which is said to have 2.3 children. Anyone who thought that would have misunderstood the sentence entirely. The logical structure of (1) is exhibited by:

(2) The number of children divided by the number of families = 2.3.

(1) is simply a short way of expressing (2), and (2) is a long-division sum. It is of the form 'a/b = c', not 'Fa'.

According to the quantifier view the surface grammar of 'Obama exists' is also misleading: 'exists' is functioning not as a predicate but as a quantifier. Quantifiers are words that denote quantity. In sentences such as 'all men are bald', 'some men are bald', 'no man is bald', 'most men are bald', the words 'all', 'some', 'no' and 'most' are **quantifiers**. The logical structure of quantified sentences was discovered by the German logician Gottlob Frege in the 19th century, and that structure is not subject–predicate.

The logical form of 'Bill is bald' can be represented as 'Ba', where 'B' denotes the property of baldness and 'a' denotes Bill. But the logical form of, e.g., 'some men are bald' is represented as $\exists x(Mx \ \& \ Bx)$, where 'M' abbreviates 'is male' and 'B' abbreviates 'is bald'. In English: there is an object x – there is at least one object x – such that x is male and bald. 'All men are bald' is represented as $(x)(Mx \rightarrow Bx)$. In English: for all objects x, if x is male then x is bald. 'Some' is known as the existential quantifier; 'all' is the universal quantifier.

The central claim of the quantifier view is that the predicate 'exists' is a disguised existential quantifier. So though the grammatical structure of 'Obama exists' is subject–predicate, it's logical stucture is represented as $\exists x(x = Obama)$ (i.e., there is an object x such that x is identical to Obama). On this view what makes it true that Obama exists is simply Obama, not the possession by Obama of the property of existence. So whereas, e.g., 'Obama is 6' tall' attributes a property to Obama, 'Obama exists' does no such thing. In general, to say 'A exists' is to say that there is an object identical to A; it is not to attribute any property to A. On this view, existence has no essence or nature. Nor is 'exists' ambiguous: different kinds of thing exist (humans, numbers, trees, rocks etc), but there are not different concepts of existence.

The quantifier view treats our other existential sentences in like fashion. 'Tigers exist' is represented as $\exists x(x \text{ is a tiger})$ (i.e., there is at least one tiger); 'Santa Claus does not exist' is represented as $\sim\exists x(x = Santa Claus)$ (i.e., it's not the case that something is identical to Santa Claus); and finally 'unicorns do not exist' is represented as $\sim\exists x(x$ is a unicorn) (i.e., it's not the case that there is a unicorn). These all seem intuitively acceptable renderings. Still the matter is hardly settled. What considerations might help decide between the property and quantifier views?

Deciding between the property and quantifier views

(i)   Historically both views have had their defenders. Meinong famously defended the property view, holding that some objects possess the property of existence, while other objects (the round square, the golden mountain, Pegasus, etc.) lack the property of existence (these are the non-existent objects). We will examine Meinong's view in more detail below.

Hume, Kant and Frege all famously rejected the property view. Hume claimed that 'the idea of existence is nothing different from the idea of any object.'[1] This claim was echoed in Kant: '[B]y whatever and however many predicates we may think of a thing – even if we completely determine it – we do not make the least addition to the thing when we further declare that this thing is.'[2]

(ii) The quantifier view is often glossed as the view that 'exists' denotes a second-level property, a property of concepts rather than objects. To say 'tigers exist' is to say that the concept *tiger* is instantiated. However, I do not understand the quantifier view in this way. On that view, 'tigers exist' is about tigers not concepts. The quantifier view is essentially the view of W.V.O. Quine.[3] The second-level property view is associated with G. Frege.[4] Despite their differences, however, I take Frege and Quine to be allies against the property view.

(iii) Take the simplest possible case – a true positive singular existential sentence such as 'Obama exists'. On both views, the sentences 'Obama exists' and '$\exists x(x = \text{Obama})$' have the same truth-value in all possible circumstances. (The views differ over whether the latter sentence displays the logical structure of the former.) So what is gained by, in addition, postulating existence as one of Obama's properties? It is a purely formal property and does no causal or explanatory work. The weight and height of Obama are causally efficacious properties, but his existence is not (although, trivially, he would not have any properties unless he existed). The postulation of a property of existence is otiose.

(iv) Consider the case of true negative existential sentences such as 'Santa Claus does not exist' and 'unicorns do not exist'. These sentences pose a familiar and ancient metaphysical puzzle. Since they are true sentences, they must be true of something (Santa Claus and unicorns, respectively). Santa Claus and unicorns must exist in order for something to be true of them. But if they exist then the sentences cannot be true. Yet we all agree they are true. Upshot: we cannot coherently embrace true negative existentials (despite the fact that there plainly are no end of such sentences).

The problem of true negative existentials

We can pose the problem in a more formal way. The rule of Existential Generalization (EG) is a valid rule in standard logic. It validates the following inference pattern:

$$\frac{...a...}{\exists x(...x...)}$$

From any sentence containing a name a, we can validly infer a sentence in which the name is replaced by variable x bound by an existential quantifier. So, e.g., from

Fred is fat

we can infer

$\exists x(x$ is fat)

In English: from 'Fred is fat' infer 'Someone is fat'. This inference certainly seems valid: how could Fred be fat without someone being fat? But if we apply (EG) to 'Santa Claus does not exist' we get:

$\exists x(x$ does not exist).

This is a contradiction: it says that there exists something which does not exist. So from the undeniable assumption that there are true negative existential sentences, together with the logical rule (EG), we can derive a contradiction. Something has gone wrong.

So far, this is a puzzle for all parties. How can defenders of the property and quantifier views respond?

The response of the quantifier view

It might be thought that there is no problem for the quantifier view, since that view would render 'Santa Claus does not exist' as $\sim\exists x(x = $ Santa Claus), where the negation appears at the front. But this is no solution. By (EG), from

$\sim \exists x(x = $ Santa Claus)

we can infer the contradiction

$\exists y\sim \exists x(x = y)$.

The best move for a defender of the quantifier view may be to eliminate names altogether, as W.V.O. Quine once suggested.[5] A sentence such as 'Plato exists' would be rendered not as $\exists x(x = $ Plato), but as $\exists x(x$ platonizes), where the predicable 'platonizes' encodes the familiar properties associated with Plato. The gain is then that 'Santa Claus does not exist' gets rendered as $\sim\exists x(x$ Santa-Clausizes). Since this (admittedly horrendous) sentence contains no names, (EG) cannot be performed upon it, thus avoiding contradiction. However, it has to be said that this manoeuvre is a controversial one.[6]

The response of the property view

What are the options on the property view? It makes no difference whether a defender of this view represents 'Santa Claus does not exist' as ~(Ea) or as (~E)a (where 'a' stands for Santa Claus and 'E' for existence). A defender of the property view who thinks that non-existence is a property as much as existence will opt for the second representation. A property theorist who does not embrace negative properties will opt for the first representation, seeing a non-existence claim as a denial of existence, rather than as the attribution of a negative property. No matter. By (EG) from ~(Ea) we may infer ∃x~(Ex), and from (~E)a we may infer ∃x(~Ex). Both conclusions are contradictions – they assert that there exists something which does not exist.

The most interesting and radical response open to defenders of the property view is to deny the validity of (EG) and embrace non-existent objects. From the truth of 'Fa' we can infer 'something is F', but 'something is F' is taken not to imply 'there exists an F'. The phrases 'there is/are', 'some', etc. are taken to have no existential import. From 'Superman does not exist' we may infer 'there is something which does not exist', but this does not imply the contradiction 'there exists an object which does not exist'. For friends of the non-existent, many things lack the property of existence, and Superman is one of them.

ALEXIUS MEINONG (1853–1920)

Alexius Meinong was an Austrian philosopher, heavily influenced by his teacher, Franz Brentano (1837–1917). From 1889 Meinong taught at the University of Graz, and made important contributions to philosophy and philosophical psychology. Meinong's philosophy of mind and metaphysics takes inspiration from Brentano's thesis that the mark of mental states is their directedness towards objects. This led Meinong to a full-blown theory of objects that embraces possible objects (the golden mountain), impossible objects (the square triangle), and incomplete objects (something tall). These objects are mind-independent, yet all are potential objects of thought. Meinong also believed in objective values, such as the good and the beautiful, detectable through emotions and desires.

• NON-EXISTENT OBJECTS

Colin McGinn is a modern defender of the view that there are non-existent objects. In a recent book he wrote:

> we find it natural to talk in the following way. Not everything that we refer to exists: Venus does, Vulcan doesn't; horses do, unicorns don't. There are merely

fictional entities as well as things that really exist. To exist is to have a property that only some of the things we refer to have – those that exist as opposed to those that are merely fictional.[7]

In propounding this view, McGinn is following in the footsteps of the Austrian philosopher Alexius Meinong, who happily embraced the non-existent and much else besides. Unlike McGinn, however, Meinong held non-existent objects to be mind-independent. These non-existent objects have a range of properties: e.g., the golden mountain has the property of being golden, Superman has the property of being a flying superhero. Of course, all non-existent objects lack the property of existence and, on views that embrace negative properties, possess the property of non-existence.

Why did Meinong hold such an extraordinary view? Here is a famous passage from Bertrand Russell:

> It is argued, e.g., by Meinong, that we can speak about 'the golden mountain', 'the round square', and so on; we can make true propositions of which these are the subjects; hence they must have some kind of logical being, since otherwise the propositions in which they occur would be meaningless. In such theories, it seems to me, there is a failure of that feeling for reality which ought to be preserved even in the most abstract studies. Logic, I should maintain, must no more admit a unicorn than zoology can; for logic is concerned with the real world just as truly as zoology, though with its more abstract and general features. To say that unicorns have an existence in heraldry, or in literature, or in imagination, is a most pitiful and paltry evasion.[8]

Four reasons to believe in non-existent objects

These quotes from McGinn and Russell suggest the following four reasons to believe in non-existent objects:

(i)   Given that definite descriptions such as 'the round square' and 'the golden mountain' are meaningful, they must denote objects. Since neither the round square nor the golden mountain exist, those descriptions must denote non-existent objects.

(ii) From the fact that definite descriptions such as 'the round square' and 'the golden mountain' feature as grammatical subjects in true sentences (such as 'the golden mountain is golden'), it follows that there is a golden mountain (though it fails to exist).

(iii) We frequently refer to things which don't exist. 'Vulcan' and 'unicorns', for example, are referring terms, and we succeed in referring when we use them. But the objects referred to do not exist.

(iv) Do we not say things like 'Some superheroes can fly: Superman can, but the Hulk cannot'? We think that there are superheroes, but we don't think they exist: so superheroes are non-existent objects. Or again don't we regard the sentence 'Sherlock Holmes lived in Baker Street' as true? And how can this be true unless there is a fictional (i.e., non-existent) object Sherlock Holmes?

Let's deal with these points in turn. (i) is not compelling. Why would anyone think that, to be meaningful, a definite description has to denote an object? A definite description, such as 'the golden mountain' or 'the largest prime number' or 'the Fountain of Youth', is a semantically complex expression whose meaning derives from the meanings of its parts and their mode of combination. We can account for the meaning of such expressions without having to postulate objects as their meanings.

(ii) is potentially more worrying. If there really were true sentences containing 'the golden mountain' as a subject term (leaving aside the negative existential case), then we would have to acknowledge that there is a golden mountain. An alleged example is: 'the golden mountain is golden'. But should we accept that this is true? In response to Meinong, and for other reasons, Russell developed his Theory of Descriptions, a theory still widely accepted today. The gist of Russell's theory was that definite descriptions (expressions of the form 'the so-and-so') were not referring terms but disguised existential quantifiers.

According to Russell's theory, a sentence of the form:

The F is G

has the following structure:

$$\exists x(Fx \ \& \ (y)(Fy \rightarrow x = y) \ \& \ Gx).$$

That is: there is exactly one thing which is F and whatever is F is G. The apparent **singular term** 'the F' 'disappears' upon analysis. The logical structure of 'The F is G' contains no place for referring terms and consists only of quantification, predication and identity.

Russell's theory implies that, where nothing is uniquely F, 'The F is G' is simply false. This means that Meinong is not entitled to treat it as a datum that a sentence like 'the golden mountain is golden' is true. On Russell's theory, this sentence says: there is exactly one golden mountain, and whatever is a golden mountain is golden. Since there is no golden mountain, 'the golden mountain is golden' is false. This disposes of the second line of argument.

RUSSELL'S THEORY OF DESCRIPTIONS

In his famous, but difficult, paper 'On Denoting' (*Mind*, 1905) Bertrand Russell put forward his Theory of Descriptions. According to this theory, descriptions – both definite (e.g., 'the author of *Waverley*') and indefinite (e.g., 'a man') – are disguised quantified phrases. Although they are grammatically subject terms, their function in complete sentences is not to refer to particular objects, but to express a condition which may or may not be satisfied by a particular object, and which could have been satisfied by different objects. Thus the sentence 'the author of *Waverley* is Scotch' is held to express a general or object-independent proposition, *viz.*, exactly one man wrote *Waverley* and whoever wrote *Waverley* is Scotch. This sentence would have expressed the very same proposition had someone other than Sir Walter Scott written *Waverley*, or had the book never been written. In contrast, the first-person pronoun 'I' is a genuine referring term. If X utters 'I am happy', the proposition expressed – in the actual situation or in other counterfactual situations – concerns only X and X's emotional state. X's utterance expresses an object-dependent proposition. Russell argued that his theory of descriptions solved a number of puzzles in the philosophy of language and mind, and enabled us to circumvent the arduous trek through Meinong's jungle.

What of (iii) and (iv)? The thought behind (iii) is that 'Vulcan' and 'unicorn' are referring terms, just like 'Mercury' and 'tiger', and so all four terms must refer to something. But here we can draw an intuitive distinction. Certainly all four terms belong in the semantic category of referring terms. But why should we accept that all four terms succeed in referring to something? Why can't there be empty referring terms (like the address of a house that no longer exists)?

The astronomer Jean Leverrier introduced the name 'Vulcan' to refer to a planet between Mercury and the Sun, the presence of which would explain certain astronomical observations. It turned out that there was no such planet. 'Vulcan' is a paradigm case of reference-failure, not a case of reference to a non-existent object. To invent a name, whether in a fictional context or some other, does not guarantee any object as referent.

The thought behind (iv) is that there are sentences we regard as true, and their truth commits us to non-existent objects. The examples given were 'Some superheroes can fly' and 'Sherlock Holmes lived in Baker Street'. It is assumed that these sentences are true and, since neither superheroes nor Sherlock Holmes exists, it is concluded that there are non-existent objects.

But we can reasonably deny that these sentences are true. Strictly speaking, they are false.[9] We only think they are true because we confuse them with related sentences which are true: e.g., 'In the Marvel comics, some superheroes can fly' or 'In Conan Doyle's stories, Holmes lived in Baker Street'. The truth of these sentences does not commit us to non-existent objects, any more than our acknowledging the truth of 'Billy believes that Santa will come tonight' commits us to believing in Santa Claus.

Why not to believe in non-existent objects

The thesis that there are non-existent objects lacks any plausible motivation. At heart, it rests on the confused idea that to any representation (e.g., in language or pictures) there must correspond an object represented. But this is an idea that has nothing to be said for it. Moreover, the idea that there are non-existent objects encounters two obvious worries: (i) where are these non-existent objects located?, and (ii) how can something which does not exist have any properties?

In consequence, we can reject non-existent objects and hold on to the intuitive equivalence between 'some/there are' and 'exists': to say that some Fs are G is to say that there exist Fs which are G. This is just as well since it was never clear what the phrases 'some/there are' meant if not 'there exists'.

NON-EXISTENT OBJECTS

Some philosophers (e.g., Meinong and his followers) believe in non-existent objects. That is, they believe that there are objects which do not exist. This thesis avoids contradiction only if 'there are' is distinguished from 'there exists'. But then we are left with the problem of explaining what 'there are' means if not 'there exists'. Why do these philosophers hold that there are non-existent objects? Because we can speak of, think about and refer to a range of things, and some of those things do not exist. We can speak of unicorns, think about Sherlock Holmes, refer to Vulcan. Hence there are such objects to be spoken of, thought about and referred to – but they do not exist. However, this is simply a confusion between the representation and the represented: not every representation represents a real object.

• CONCLUDING REMARKS

The central debate about existence is that between the property and quantifier views. Since the quantifier view is no less explanatory than the property view, and does not postulate an otiose property of existence, it is to be preferred. In rejecting the property view, we should also reject its more egregious kin: the doctrine of non-existent objects and the view that all meaningful names and descriptions refer to something.

Our rejection of the property view has implications for other areas of philosophy. Some versions of the Ontological Argument presuppose the property view, and can be criticized on that account. One example is Descartes' version of the Ontological

Argument, presented in his Fifth Meditation.[10] Descartes' argument runs: my idea of God is the idea of a being with all the perfections; necessary existence is a perfection; so God (necessarily) exists. This argument does seem to presuppose that existence (or necessary existence) is one of God's properties.

• STUDY QUESTIONS

- Is existence a property of Fido, alongside loyalty and friendliness?
- Should we countenance non-existent objects?
- Does Anselm's version of the Ontological Argument presuppose the property view of existence? If not, why not? (See Chapter 1.)

• ANNOTATED FURTHER READING

C. McGinn, *Logical Properties* (Oxford: Oxford University Press, 2000). McGinn's chapter 'Existence' provides a clear statement of a contemporary Meinongian position.

P. van Inwagen, 'McGinn on Existence', *Philosophical Quarterly*, 58 (2008), pp. 36–58. A clear and insightful critique of McGinn's Meinongianism.

W.V.O. Quine, 'On What There Is', in his *Two Dogmas of Empiricism* (New York: Harper & Row, 1963), pp. 1–20. A classic paper. Quine supports Russell against Meinong.

• INTERNET RESOURCES

P. Mackie (1998), 'Existence', *Routledge Encyclopedia of Philosophy*, ed. E. Craig. Retrieved 31 May 2006 from <http://www.rep.routledge.com/article/X013>.

Johann Marek, 'Alexius Meinong', *The Stanford Encyclopedia of Philosophy* (Summer 2009 Edition), ed. Edward N. Zalta, URL = <http://plato.stanford.edu/archives/sum2009/entries/meinong/>.

B. Miller, (2002), 'Existence', *The Stanford Encyclopedia of Philosophy* (Summer 2002 edition), ed. Edward N. Zalta. Retrieved 31 May 2006 from <http://plato.stanford.edu/archives/sum2002/entries/existence>.

M. Reicher, 'Non-Existent Objects', *The Stanford Encyclopedia of Philosophy* ed. Edward N. Zalta. http://plato.stanford.edu/entries/nonexistent-objects/

Sorensen, Roy, 'Nothingness', *The Stanford Encyclopedia of Philosophy* (Spring 2009 Edition), ed. Edward N. Zalta, URL = <http://plato.stanford.edu/archives/spr2009/entries/nothingness/>.

• NOTES

1. D. Hume, *A Treatise of Human Nature*, ed. L.A. Selby-Bigge (Oxford: Oxford University Press, 1951), p.94.
2. I. Kant, *Critique of Pure Reason*, ed. N. Kemp-Smith (London: Macmillan, 1929), B628.
3. W.V.O. Quine, *Word and Object* (Cambridge, Mass.: MIT Press, 1960).
4. G. Frege, (1884), *Die Grundlagen der Arithmetik*. English translation: J.L. Austin, *The Foundations of Arithmetic* (Oxford: Blackwell, second revised edition, 1974).
5. See 'On What There Is', reprinted in *From a Logical Point of View* (New York: Harper & Row, 1963).
6. Saul Kripke's view of names stands in opposition to Quine's view. See Kripke's *Naming and Necessity* (Oxford: Basil Blackwell, 1980).
7. C. McGinn, *Logical Properties* (Oxford: Oxford University Press, 2000), p. 16.
8. B. Russell, 'Descriptions', in his *Introduction to Mathematical Philosophy* (New York: Simon & Schuster, 1961), p. 169.
9. On some views, sentences such as 'Some superheroes can fly' and 'Sherlock Holmes lived in Baker Street' are made true by (existent) abstract objects. But how can an abstract object bend a poker, smoke a pipe or fly through the air?
10. See R. Descartes, *Meditations on First Philosophy*, trans, and ed. J, Cottingham (Cambridge: Cambridge University Press, 1996).

4

modality

<hr>

• INTRODUCTION

'Modality', as that term is used by contemporary philosophers and logicians, is the name given to the study of possibility and necessity.[1] A **modal** claim is any claim which contains words such as 'possibly' or 'necessarily' or cognate expressions such as 'essential', 'accidental', 'might', 'must', 'could', 'would', etc.

We are concerned here with **metaphysical modality**, i.e., modality grounded in the identity and nature of things. We are not concerned with the so-called epistemic modalities. Asked whether the Raiders won last night's game, I reply (unhelpfully) 'they might have done'. This use of 'might' merely indicates that a Raiders' victory is consistent with everything I know. In this chapter we are not interested in such epistemic uses of modal words.

We will start by looking at the ancient distinction between essential and accidental properties, the very intelligibility of which has been called into question, and then look at the broader project of understanding necessary truth, including possible worlds analyses.

• ESSENTIALISM

The distinction between essential and accidental properties derives, like so much in metaphysics, from Aristotle. The idea is that some of the properties of an object or **natural kind** are essential; others accidental. So it may be that Socrates is essentially human but accidentally bald, or that tigers are essentially animals but accidentally striped. It is part of the identity and nature of Socrates that he is human, but not that he is bald. It is part of the identity and nature of tigers that they are animals, but not that they are striped. Intuitively, if x is essentially F then x is necessarily F, and if x is accidentally G then x is contingently G (i.e., x is G but might not have been).

Quine's doubts

Philosophers, especially those in the **empiricist** tradition, are suspicious of so-called **de re** necessity (where a property is said to hold necessarily of a particular object or natural kind), and regard the only legitimate variety of necessity as that which holds of sentences or propositions (so-called **de dicto** necessity). A.J. Ayer, B. Russell and

W.V.O. Quine are prime examples of such philosophers. Quine was the most vigorous prosecutor of this case.

Defenders of *de re* modality commit themselves to 'Aristotelian essentialism', the doctrine that:

> [A]n object, of itself and by whatever name or none, must be seen as having some of its traits necessarily and others contingently.[2]

Quine thought Aristotelian essentialism incoherent, and held that whether an object has a property essentially or not depends on how that object is named or described. Why did Quine hold this view?

A famous passage from *Word and Object* contains the following argument:

> Mathematicians may conceivably be said to be necessarily rational and not necessarily two-legged; and cyclists necessarily two-legged and not necessarily rational. But what of an individual who counts among his eccentricities both mathematics and cycling? Is this concrete individual necessarily rational and contingently two-legged or vice versa? Just insofar as we are talking referentially of the object, with no special bias towards a background grouping of mathematicians as against cyclists or vice versa, there is no semblance of sense in rating some of his attributes as necessary and others contingent.[3]

What exactly is the argument here? Its conclusion is clear enough: it makes no sense to say of Cyril, our cycling mathematician, that he is necessarily rational and contingently two-legged, or vice versa. What we can say is that considered as a mathematician, Cyril is necessarily rational and contingently two-legged; but considered as a cyclist, he is contingently rational and necessarily two-legged. It makes no sense to say of Cyril himself (Cyril unconsidered) that he is necessarily one thing or another.

ESSENTIALISM

Essentialism is the metaphysical view, originating in Aristotle, that objects (such as Socrates and Edinburgh) and natural kinds (such as water and tigers) have some properties essentially and others accidentally. It is controversial which properties are essential, but here are some plausible examples: Socrates is essentially human, Edinburgh is essentially a city, water is essentially H_2O, and tigers are essentially animals. Baldness, in contrast, is an accidental property of Socrates. Essentialist claims, though intuitive, have often been attacked, especially by empiricists. Quine, for example, led a spirited campaign against essentialism last century, but his attack was, arguably, ill-conceived. Interesting essentialist truths, such as those above, are not known *a priori*; they are the result of empirical investigation. Yet they are necessary. How can we have empirical knowledge of necessities? Saul Kripke provided a theoretical framework in which we can make sense of empirically known necessities.

Reply to Quine

The argument for Quine's conclusion is contained in his opening sentence. Concede this and his conclusion follows. So how should an essentialist respond? Essentialists hold that objects (however named or described or considered) have some properties essentially, others accidentally. Different kinds of object will have different essential properties. Cyril, like other cyclists and mathematicians, is a human being. It is plausible to suppose that rationality is an essential property of human beings, while being two-legged is not.

In that case, an essentialist can claim that Quine's opening sentence is false since its second conjunct is false. Cyclists, like all other human beings, are necessarily rational and only contingently two-legged. Of course, it's true that necessarily all cyclists are two-legged. But this *de dicto* truth is consistent with the *de re* truth that any actual cyclist might not have been two-legged (and hence not have been a cyclist). Analogy: necessarily all husbands are married, but any particular husband might not have been married.

It may seem that we have a stand-off between Quine and the essentialist. But that is not so. Quine assumes as a datum a premise which no essentialist would allow. So Quine's argument begs the question. We have been given no reason to think that Aristotelian essentialism is ill-conceived.

• VARIETIES OF ESSENTIALISM

Pending further anti-essentialist arguments, let us take the notion of an essential property to be coherent. Many further questions remain. Do **concrete** objects in space and time, **abstract** objects outside space and time, natural kinds, sets and properties all have essential properties? Does every entity (object, property, fact, event) have some essential properties? Which properties are essential?

Leibniz held that all properties of an object are essential. The opposite view would be that all properties are accidental. Both views are implausible. Surely I might not have worn a jacket yesterday. So, *contra* Leibniz, some properties (like *wearing a jacket*) are accidental. Surely the number 2 must be even. So, *contra* the anti-essentialist, some properties (like *being even*) are essential.

So let us take essentialism to be the view that some properties of an object or kind are essential, others accidental. How do we decide which properties are essential? Some entities, such as sets and numbers, are defined by various principles of individuation (e.g., a set is defined by its members, the number 3 is defined by its relations to other numbers, etc.), thereby yielding essential properties.

In the case of concrete, contingent objects such as you and me, and natural kinds such as water and cats, essentialist claims have recently been advanced and defended by

Saul Kripke.[4] The varieties of essentialism which Kripke and others have found plausible include:

- *Sortal essentialism*: the most fundamental sort or classification that a thing falls under – it does so essentially. So if Fido is a dog, then Fido is essentially a dog.
- *Constitution essentialism*: whatever material makes up a concrete object does so essentially. So if my desk is made of wood, it is essentially made of wood.
- *Origin essentialism*: an object could not have had an origin radically different from its actual origin. So Hitler essentially came from the sperm and egg he in fact came from.
- *Kind essentialism*: when science discovers the nature of a kind or species, it reveals the essential nature of that kind. So if gold is the element with atomic number 79, it is so essentially; if water is H_2O then water is essentially H_2O; if cats are animals, they are essentially animals.

These four broad varieties of essentialist claims have interesting implications. For example, though necessary, they are known on the basis of experience. It was an empirical discovery that, e.g., water is composed of H_2O molecules or that cats are animals. Yet these truths are necessary. Kripke was the first to point out this feature and thus to break the previously dominant identification of the necessary with the *a priori*. Some necessary truths are knowable only through experience.

Of course, this result assumes that essentialist claims in the above categories are true. What could be said to a sceptic who, while not entertaining Quine's doubts about the coherence of essential properties, is unconvinced by any of the just mooted essentialist claims? This highlights the basic epistemic problem with essentialist claims. We know how to determine whether x is F (e.g., go and look, if F is an observable feature). But having determined that x is F, how do we then determine whether x *must be* F? Arguments have been given in particular cases (e.g., for essentiality of origin and kind essentialism) but the central intuition concerns the loss of the subject if essentialism is rejected.[5]

For example, a defender of sortal essentialism holds that Socrates, since human, is essentially human. His anti-essentialist opponent denies this, and holds that Socrates might have failed to be human, and might have been pretty much anything – a poached egg, a doorknob, a Rolls Royce, a Siamese cat, etc. But we have a hard time imagining these possibilities as possibilities *for* Socrates. Rather the possibilities for Socrates seem fixed by his nature as a human being. Accordingly, we can understand that Socrates might have been a carpenter or a used-chariot salesman, might have died in infancy, or might have been a dwarf. For the same reason, we cannot understand the suggestion that Socrates might have been a poached egg or a Rolls Royce. These are not possibilities for a human being. Plausibility, it seems, lies with the essentialist.

• NECESSARY TRUTH

Two theories

What makes true our modal truths?

(i)   One theory is the logical theory of necessity:

> (LTN) Necessarily P is true just if P is logically true; possibly P is true just if P is not logically false.

Logical truths are, e.g., truths of the form 'P or not-P' or 'if P then P'. But neither 'Socrates is human' nor 'water is H_2O' are truths of logic. (LTN) would rob us of our plausible essentialist claims. On (LTN) Socrates might not have been human and water might not have been H_2O.

When we say that Socrates is essentially human or that water is essentially H_2O, the necessity involved is metaphysical not logical. It is grounded in the natures of Socrates and water. (LTN) cannot capture these metaphysical notions of necessity and possibility.

(ii)   In contrast, the conceivability theory attempts to understand necessity in terms of inconceivability, and possibility in terms of conceivability:

> (CTN) Necessarily P just if not-P is inconceivable; possibly P just if P is conceivable.

But there are problems with (CTN). To start with: conceivable by whom? Different people can conceive different things, yet possibility is not person-relative. Maybe it means: conceivable by someone. But presumably some feats of conceiving are beyond the capacities of any actual person; yet possibilities should not be thus limited. If we appeal to the imaginative capacities of *possible* persons we are embroiled in circularity.

Further, what rules out conceiving the impossible? If it is ruled out by *fiat*, then we are using possibility to analyse conceivability ('only what is possible is conceivable'). If it is not ruled out, perhaps impossibilities are conceivable (hence (CTN) is false). For example, maybe circular time is conceivable, yet (because of the nature of time) impossible. Conversely, there may be possibilities (or even actualities) – e.g., concerning the nature of space-time or the origin of the universe – which are inconceivable.

W.V.O. QUINE (1908–2000)

Quine was one of the most dominant figures in Anglo-American philosophy during the 20th century. After receiving his BA from Oberlin College in 1930 and his PhD from Harvard in 1932, Quine spent his entire working life at Harvard. He wrote a number of logic textbooks, but also many influential articles and books in the philosophy of language, epistemology and **ontology**. Quine came to prominence after the publication of his landmark essay 'Two Dogmas of Empiricism' in 1952. This was not, as its title might suggest, an anti-empiricist tract, but a plea for a more radical empiricism, in which traditional distinctions (analytic/synthetic, necessary/contingent, *a priori*/empirical) are re-conceptualized as ones of degree rather than kind.

This re-conceptualization in turn allowed Quine to formulate his coherentist picture of knowledge in the final section of 'Two Dogmas', according to which any sentence could be revised, or held true, provided suitable adjustments were made elsewhere in one's system of beliefs. No sentence is immune to revision in virtue of what it means; hence there are no analytic sentences, as traditionally understood. Quine's coherentist picture also yields a view of philosophy as continuous with the sciences. Just as there are no analytic sentences, so there is no 'first philosophy', no category of philosophical truths verifiable independently of one's total picture of the world. This view of philosophy was very influential, especially in the United States.

Ayer and Quine on necessary truth

In the early part of the 20th century, many philosophers thought that all necessary truths were **analytic** (i.e., true in virtue of meaning). A.J. Ayer (1936) wrote that:

> necessary propositions ... are without exception analytic propositions. ... [T]he reason why they cannot be confuted in experience is that they do not make any assertions about the empirical world. They simply record our determination to use words in a certain fashion.[6]

This view, typical of its time, regarded necessity and possibility as linguistic phenomena. Necessary truths are the result of convention, and hence analytic. Thus '9 is greater than 7' or 'all vixens are foxes' are necessary because true in virtue of the meanings of the contained words.

W.V.O. Quine rejected Ayer's analysis. In his famous 1952 article 'Two Dogmas of Empiricism' Quine criticized the notion of analyticity, used so freely by Ayer.[7] Empiricists prior to Quine had assumed that all truths could be cleanly divided into two camps: either {analytic, necessary and *a priori*} or {synthetic, contingent and empirical}. Quine argued that there were no such hard and fast distinctions. What previous philosophers had thought of as differences in kind were merely differences of degree. There is no class of sentences (those true in virtue of meaning) which are categorically different from all other sentences (those true in virtue of meaning and the world).[8] Hence no sentence is immune from revision in virtue of its meaning. All sentences are revisable.

To label an accepted sentence 'analytic' or 'necessary' or '*a priori*' indicates only one thing: to give up that sentence (to come to regard it as false) would involve considerable disruption to one's web of belief. In giving up, e.g., 'all metals expand when heated' or 'objects fall towards the earth' one would have to give up much else besides. But, however disruptive it may be, any sentence can, in principle, be revised if sufficient compensating changes are made elsewhere.

Although an enemy of *de re* necessity, Quine can make some sense of *de dicto* necessity: to say 'necessarily 9 is greater than 7' is to indicate that giving up the sentence '9 is greater than 7' would entrain massive revisions elsewhere in one's system of beliefs. That is all the adverb 'necessarily' indicates; it does not assign any kind of protected status.

Criticisms of Ayer and Quine

The theories of Ayer and Quine have been subject to many criticisms. Thanks to Saul Kripke's 1970 series of lectures (later published as *Naming and Necessity*) Ayer's case for identifying necessity with analyticity has collapsed. Kripke's theory of proper names and natural kind terms provided plausible examples of necessary truths which are not analytic (e.g., 'Tully is Cicero', 'Hesperus is Phosphorus', 'water is H_2O', etc.).

Quine's arguments in 'Two Dogmas' have been subjected to much criticism over the years.[9] Here is one problem. Is Quine entitled to the notion of revisability? I can be said to have revised a sentence S just if I once accepted S, and now reject S (or vice versa). But of course this assumes that the two occurrences of S have the same meaning – otherwise no revision would have taken place. But Quine is as critical of the notion of sameness of meaning as he is of analyticity, necessity, etc. In which case, Quine cannot help himself to the notion of revisability, and cannot consistently advance his radical thesis that all sentences are revisable.

Moreover, it is plain that some sentences are not revisable, in the ordinary sense of that word. How, holding the meaning of the sentence constant, could I come to regard, e.g., 'all triangles have three sides' as false?

Possible worlds accounts

The notion of a possible world was made popular by Leibniz, who argued – in his *Theodicy* (1710) – that our world, having been created by God, is the best of all possible worlds. In the 1950s and 60s developments in modal logic led to a renewed interest in possible worlds. The schematic idea is simple enough:

(i) Necessarily P **if and only if** P is true in all possible worlds.

(ii) Possibly P if and only if P is true in some possible world(s).

So 'necessarily 9 is greater than 7' is understood as 'in all possible worlds 9 is greater than 7'. 'Socrates might have been a carpenter' is rendered as 'possibly Socrates is a carpenter' which in turn is understood as 'in some possible world(s) Socrates is a carpenter'.

But whether (i) and (ii) illuminate our notions of necessity and possibility depends on how we understand talk of possible worlds. It might be thought that such talk is merely a picturesque way of representing necessities and possibilities. After all, our judgement that there is a possible world in which P seems entirely parasitic upon our ordinary modal judgement: possibly P. We have no independent access to possible worlds. We cannot look through any metaphysical telescope to determine how things are in other possible worlds.

However, some hold that possible worlds talk, properly understood, can yield theoretical insight into our modal notions.

Actualism

According to actualists, talk of possible worlds can be preserved, but without any serious ontological commitment to possible worlds or possible objects. The only concrete world is the actual world; other possible worlds are constructs out of actual objects, sentences, propositions, properties or states of affairs. All modal truths have to be accounted for in terms of actual resources. A difficult case for actualists concerns the possibility of 'aliens' – e.g., novel chemical elements or novel fundamental properties. Aliens seem possible, but how are they to be accounted for from only actual materials?

Actualists (such as Saul Kripke) tend to play down the so-called problem of 'transworld identification'.[10] According to the actualist, in glossing 'Nixon might have been Russian' as 'there is a possible world in which Nixon is Russian' we don't have to identify an individual in some (non-actual) possible world as Nixon. We have already stipulated that world to contain Nixon, so no question of identification arises.

Possibilism

Possibilists, on the other hand, hold that there are possible worlds and possible objects (alien and non-alien). Standard possibilists take only actual objects to exist and so regard (merely) possible objects as non-existent. They think that there are possible objects (the sister I might have had, the possible fat man in the doorway, etc.), but take them not to exist. Standard possibilism thus encounters the objections (outlined in Chapter 3) to the doctrine of non-existent objects.

However, David Lewis is a non-standard possibilist who holds that possible worlds and objects exist in the very same way that the actual world and its objects exist. He thus avoids the objections to standard possibilism. His view is known as modal **realism**.

DAVID LEWIS (1941–2002)

David Lewis taught briefly at UCLA before moving to Princeton University in 1970. Lewis wrote on many areas of philosophy, but is best known for his work on **counterfactual conditionals** and the philosophy of modality (possibility and necessity). According to Lewis, a counterfactual conditional of the form 'if A had been the case, B would have been the case' is true just if some possible world where A and B are both true is 'closer' to our world than any world where A and not-B are both true. Lewis takes 'closeness' to be matter of similarity and takes a realist view of possible worlds. Possible worlds exist in just the way that our world exists. There is nothing special or privileged about the actual world, since each world is actual to its inhabitants. Some have complained that 'closeness' cannot be understood in terms of similarity, and many have complained that Lewis's realist view of possible objects and possible worlds is incredible. Lewis asks us to believe that golden mountains and talking donkeys exist (in other worlds) in just the way that our mountains and donkeys exist.

• MODAL REALISM

Lewis writes:

> I advocate a thesis of plurality of worlds, or modal realism, which holds that our world is one world among others. There are countless other worlds, other very inclusive things. ... They are isolated: there are no spatiotemporal relations at all between different things that belong to different worlds. Nor does anything that happens at one world cause anything to happen at another. ... The other worlds are of a kind with this world of ours. ... Nor does this world differ from others in its manner of existing. ... The worlds are not of our own making.[11]

It is important to appreciate that the doctrine of modal realism is not the view that 'many worlds actually exist' (a view sometimes proposed by certain interpreters of quantum mechanics). On such a view, the actual world is much bigger than we think it is. That is not Lewis's view. Nor, as noted above, is modal realism the view that there are possible worlds or possible objects which do not exist. Lewis draws no distinction between 'there are Fs' and 'Fs exist'.

Lewis does not believe in non-existent objects, but he does think that possible objects exist as much as actual objects. The set of actual objects is but a small subset of all existing objects. Actual existence (existing in the actual world) is not in any way privileged. It is not the mark of the real since other worlds are equally real. The word 'actual' uttered by the inhabitant of any world simply refers to the world of the inhabitant.

Possible worlds are concrete like our world, irreducible to anything else (e.g., to abstract objects such as sets of propositions). Possible worlds are spatio-temporal unities, and spatio-temporally isolated from each other. Thus possible worlds are not any spatial or temporal distance from each other.

Though not a reductionist about possible worlds, Lewis is a reductionist about necessity and possibility. He thinks that modality can be understood in non-modal terms. As an empiricist, he construes necessity as a form of regularity. Necessity is a matter of regularity across all the concrete worlds (necessarily p just if p holds in all the worlds).

De re modal claims

There is a problem for modal realism in the case of *de re* predications of actual individuals. One might have thought that the sentence 'Socrates might have been a carpenter' would be rendered as 'there is a possible world in which Socrates is a carpenter', where the latter is made true by the existence of a concrete world, distinct from our world, in which Socrates is a carpenter. But that requires either that Socrates exists in both that world and our world (and in many others) or else that Socrates is a super-entity composed of all his world-parts (so that only parts of the **five-dimensional** Socrates exist in various possible worlds). Neither alternative is congenial to common sense.

For Lewis, as for Leibniz, individuals are world-bound; hence there are no transworld identities. Socrates exists in our world and in no other. What then makes true 'Socrates might have been a carpenter'? Lewis's answer: a world containing a counterpart of Socrates (someone similar to Socrates in relevant respects) who is a carpenter. Similarly, Socrates is essentially human if and only if all counterparts of Socrates are human. Counterpart theory thus allows Lewis to avoid the fate that would otherwise befall world-bound theories: *viz.*, counting all properties of an individual as essential. (A consequence that Leibniz happily embraced.)

One motivation for counterpart theory

Here is one reason to prefer counterpart relations to transworld identities. It is plausible to suppose (i) an artefact such as a boat could have been made from a slightly different set of planks, but (ii) not from a completely different set (see Origin essentialism above). Suppose that my actual boat B is made from 100 planks.

If we think in terms of transworld identities, then, by (i), we can postulate a world w1 in which B was made of 99 of the original planks, plus one extra. Call the ship in w1,

B1. Applying (i) to B1 yields w2 in which B1 is composed of 98 of the original planks, plus two extra. Call the ship in w2, B2. And so on. By repeated applications of (i), we end up with w100 in which B100 is composed of none of the original planks. Since identity is **transitive**, and since B = B1, B1 = B2 ... B99 = B100, it follows that B = B100, contrary to (ii). Hence transworld identity, (i) and (ii) are incompatible; yet (i) and (ii) are plausible principles.

Counterpart theory can endorse (i) and (ii) without contradiction. Since the counterpart relation (like any similarity relation) is not transitive, the counterpart theorist can concede that B and B1 are counterparts, B1 and B2 are counterparts ... B99 and B100 are counterparts, but deny that B and B100 are counterparts. Hence, we have a reason to prefer counterpart relations to transworld identity.

A famous objection to counterpart theory

Nonetheless, counterpart theory has its critics. In *Naming and Necessity* Saul Kripke denounced counterpart theory for completely failing to capture the content of *de re* modal claims. According to counterpart theory, x's possibly being F consists in x having a counterpart – a relevantly similar object in another possible world – that is F. Kripke claimed that this cannot be right. Humphrey cares that he might have won the 1968 presidential election, but he 'could not care less whether someone else, no matter how much resembling him, would have been victorious in another possible world'.[12] Or again, I care that I might have been killed by a stray bullet, but may be indifferent to the shooting of someone similar to me in a world spatio-temporally unrelated to our world. Opinion is still divided over whether Kripke's objection hits its target.[13]

Assessing modal realism

Lewis's modal realism has things to be said in its favour. His concrete worlds provide the truthmakers for our modal claims. 'Pigs might fly' is true because there is a bit of reality (spatio-temporally unconnected to us) in which pigs fly. And the mystery of why our world is life-permitting disappears. Many worlds are life-permitting and ours happens to be one of them. (See Chapter 1.)

However, Lewis's modal realism faces major objections. Here are four:

(i) Lewis holds that each possible world is a unified spatio-temporal whole, spatio-temporally isolated from every other world. He thus cannot allow that there are, or even might have been, abstract objects. There cannot be abstract objects in our world since their spatio-temporal isolation from concrete objects would immediately disqualify them from being part of our world. This is a problem if there are good reasons to believe in abstract objects, such as numbers or Platonic universals.

(ii) It is not clear that Lewis's framework can account for all possibilities. One possibility is the null possibility: the possibility that there might have been nothing.

Lewis cannot accommodate this possibility. For Lewis, a world is a spatio-temporal whole and must contain something:

> just some homogeneous unoccupied space-time, or maybe only one single point of it. ... That makes it necessary that there is something.[14]

Intuitively, however, there might have been nothing – not just an empty possible world but nothing, no world whatsoever.

(iii) The theory is ontologically bloated. We are asked to believe that there exist countless concrete worlds, spatio-temporally unrelated to each other, containing talking donkeys, flying pigs, dragons, goblins and golden mountains, existing in just the full-blooded way that our pigs, donkeys and mountains exist. For most philosophers, this is simply too high a price to pay.

(iv) Lewis attempts a **reductive** analysis of modality: modal facts are cashed out in terms of non-modal ones. So Lewis's concrete worlds must be specifiable without using modal terms such as 'possible' or 'consistent'. The modal claim 'Socrates might have been a carpenter' is cashed out as: 'there is a concrete world, spatio-temporally unrelated to our world, in which a counterpart of Socrates is a carpenter'.

But why should existence in a concrete world spatio-temporally unconnected to our world constitute possibility? Despite Lewis's intentions, why should we not understand modal realism as tantamount to the view that the actual world is composed of a realm of spatio-temporally unconnected worlds? In which case, no account of possibility and necessity will have been provided.

A MODAL ONTOLOGICAL ARGUMENT

Alvin Plantinga proposed an ingenious modal version of the Ontological Argument discussed in Chapter 1: (1) It is possible that a **necessary being** exists; so (2) A necessary being exists. The argument is valid (at least on standard modal logic). If any possible world contains a necessary being, every world must contain that being. But why accept (1)? One might equally accept: (1*) It is possible that no necessary being exists. From (1*) it follows: (2*) A necessary being does not exist. Why accept (1) over (1*)? (1) is supported by the plausible principle: if a concept F is coherent, there is a possible world containing Fs. So if, as many would accept, *necessary being* is a coherent concept, then there is a world containing a necessary being. Consequently, a necessary being exists.

• CONCLUDING REMARKS

We have covered a lot of material in this chapter. Quine's attack on essentialism was rebuffed, and some plausible varieties of essentialism were outlined. Various theories of necessary truth were examined, including David Lewis's modal realism, and all were found to be open to serious objections. It remains to be seen whether actualist theories can provide the material to ground our modal claims.

• STUDY QUESTIONS

- How should we understand essentialist claims?
- Why did Quine reject Aristotelian essentialism?
- Which essentialist theses do you find plausible?
- How should we understand necessary truth?
- How would you defend modal realism?

• ANNOTATED FURTHER READING

R.M. Adams, 'Theories of Actuality', reprinted in *The Possible and the Actual*, ed. M. Loux (Ithaca: Cornell University Press, 1979), pp. 190–210. Defence of a version of actualism wherein possible worlds are constructed out of sets of propositions.

S. Kripke, *Naming and Necessity* (Oxford: Basil Blackwell, 1980). One of the most brilliant and influential works of contemporary philosophy. Kripke offered a philosophy of language congenial to essentialism and, in doing so, rehabilitated metaphysical inquiry as central to philosophy.

D. Lewis, *On the Plurality of Worlds* (Oxford: Basil Blackwell, 1986). Classic exposition and defence of modal realism.

A. Plantinga, 'Actualism and Possible Worlds', reprinted in *The Possible and the Actual*, ed. M. Loux (Ithaca: Cornell University Press, 1979), pp. 20–47. Defence of a version of actualism wherein possible worlds are constructed out of states of affairs.

W.V.O. Quine, 'Two Dogmas of Empiricism' (especially section 6) and 'Reference and Modality', in his *From a Logical Point of View* (New York: Harper & Row, 1963), pp. 139–60. Two classic papers defending scepticism about modal notions.

• INTERNET RESOURCES

K. Fine, 'Essence and Modality', http://philosophy.fas.nyu.edu/docs/IO/1160/essence.pdf.

Peter Hylton, 'Willard van Orman Quine', *The Stanford Encyclopedia of Philosophy* (Summer 2010 Edition), ed. Edward N. Zalta, http://plato.stanford.edu/archives/sum2010/entries/quine/.

C. Menzel, 'Actualism', *The Stanford Encyclopedia of Philosophy* (Fall 2008 Edition), ed. Edward N. Zalta, http://plato.stanford.edu/entries/actualism.

Teresa Robertson, 'Essential vs. Accidental Properties', *The Stanford Encyclopedia of Philosophy* (Fall 2008 Edition), ed. Edward N. Zalta, http://plato.stanford.edu/archives/fall2008/entries/essential-accidental/.

T. Yagisawa, 'Possible Objects', *The Stanford Encyclopedia of Philosophy* ed. Edward N. Zalta, http://plato.stanford.edu/entries/possible-objects/.

• NOTES

1. It is a good question whether, and if so in what sense or senses, possibility is prior to necessity, or vice versa. It is also a good question in epistemology whether, and if so in what sense or senses, knowledge of possibility is prior to knowledge of necessity, or vice versa. (On the latter question, see Bob Hale, 'Knowledge of Possibility and of Necessity', *Proceedings of the Aristotelian Society*, 2002, pp. 1–20). I do not address these questions here.
2. 'Reference and Modality', in his *From a Logical Point of View* (New York: Harper & Row, 1963), p. 155.
3. W.V.O. Quine, *Word and Object* (Cambridge, Mass., MIT Press, 1960), p. 199.
4. S. Kripke, *Naming and Necessity* (Oxford: Blackwell, 1980)
5. See *Naming and Necessity*, p. 114, ft 56, for a (not very convincing) argument for origin essentialism. As to kind essentialism, if 'water' and 'H_2O' are names, and the scientific discovery is the discovery that water = H_2O, then, on Kripke's semantic theory (expounded in *Naming and Necessity*), it is necessary that water = H_2O, and hence water is essentially H_2O.
6. A.J. Ayer, *Language, Truth and Logic* (Harmondsworth: Penguin, 1976), p.112.
7. 'Two Dogmas of Empiricism', in his *From a Logical Point of View* (New York: Harper & Row, 1963).
8. In 'Two Dogmas' Quine suggested that explicit stipulations (by 'X' I will mean 'Y') are an exception to this claim. It is unclear whether this is consistent with Quine's overall view.
9. Soon after its publication H.P. Grice and P.F. Strawson made some telling objections in their 'In Defence of A Dogma', *Philosophical Review*, 65 (1957), pp. 141–58.
10. S. Kripke *op. cit.*, pp. 49–53.
11. D. Lewis, *On the Plurality of Worlds* (Oxford: Basil Blackwell, 1986), pp. 2–3.
12. S. Kripke *op. cit.*, p. 45.
13. For a reply to Kripke's objection, see Allen Hazen, 'Counterpart-Theoretic Semantics for Modal Logic', *Journal of Philosophy*, Vol. 76, No. 6 (June 1979), pp. 319–38. (Hazen has his own objections to counterpart theory.) For further discussion, see G. Forbes, *The Metaphysics of Modality* (Oxford: Clarendon Press, 1985), pp. 64–70, and K. Fine's 'Critical Notice of D. Lewis's *Counterfactuals*', *Mind*, 84 (1975), pp. 451–8.
14. D. Lewis *op. cit.*, p. 73.

5

puzzles of constitution and identity

• INTRODUCTION

Metaphysics, understood in its most general sense, is concerned with the nature and identity of things. The concern, in the first instance, is with kinds of things, not particular things, though examples will inevitably involve particular things for purposes of illustration. In this chapter we will look at puzzles concerning the relation between an artefact and its matter, and between an artefact and its parts. The puzzles are interesting because of what they teach us about the relations of coincidence, constitution and identity.

• THREE PUZZLES

(i) The puzzle of the statue and the clay

On Monday a sculptor buys some clay. By Friday he has sculpted it into a statue of the biblical king David. Call the lump of clay 'Lump' and the statue 'David'. Since Lump existed before David, Lump ≠ David. On Friday, Lump and David occupy the very same space and are composed of the same matter. How can two material objects occupy the same space at the same time?

(ii) The mysterious case of Lumpl and Goliath

This case is similar to (i) but with a crucial twist. In a famous 1975 article, Allan Gibbard imagines a sculptor creating a statue of the biblical giant Goliath.[1] The sculptor fuses two pieces of clay to form a new piece, and in doing so creates the statue of Goliath. Then the following day he blows up the statue, destroying both statue and lump. Let us call the statue 'Goliath' and the lump 'Lumpl'.

Unlike David and Lump, Lumpl and Goliath existed for the same period of time (Lumpl did not exist before Goliath), occupied the same space, and were composed of the very same clay molecules. Surely we should hold that Lumpl = Goliath?

But Lumpl and Goliath seem to differ in their **modal** properties. What is possible for Lumpl is not possible for Goliath. For example, Lumpl might have been squeezed into a ball and not destroyed; but that is not a possibility for Goliath. Statues have their shape essentially; lumps do not. According to the universally accepted **Leibniz's Law**, if x = y then x and y have all properties in common. Hence, if Lumpl and Goliath fail to share all properties, they cannot be identical. (Some philosophers hold that Lumpl and Goliath differ in non-modal properties too: e.g., Goliath is beautiful, but Lumpl is not.)

So we have reason to say that Lumpl = Goliath, and reason to say that Lumpl ≠ Goliath.

(iii) The incredible voyages of the Ship of Theseus

The story of the Ship of Theseus has been used by philosophers to illustrate three quite different possibilities:

(a) The Ship of Theseus is sailing the seas and comes upon a channel too narrow for it safely to pass through. The ship is promptly dismantled, the planks carried overland, and then reassembled. We can assume that each plank was returned to its original position. Has Theseus's ship survived this process?

(b) In this scenario, the Ship of Theseus sails the seas, in regular need of repair. After a plank is removed and discarded, it is immediately replaced. The repairs are so extensive that, after a number of years, none of the original planks remains. This, as Plutarch writes:

> afforded an example to the philosophers in their disputations concerning the identity of things that are changed by addition, some contending that it was the same, and others that it was not.[2]

Did the Ship of Theseus survive the removal and replacement of all its planks or is the later ship a new ship numerically distinct from Theseus's original ship?

(c) The third scenario involves an ingenious twist on the second. Let us imagine that the removed planks are not discarded, but used to construct another ship, plank-for-plank identical with the original Ship of Theseus. One ship left to sail the seas many years ago, now two ships bob side by side in Athens harbour. Both the continuously repaired ship and the re-constituted ship have a claim to be the Ship of Theseus. But, since identity is **transitive**, the original ship cannot be identical to two distinct ships. So which of the later ships (if either) is the Ship of Theseus?

SAUL KRIPKE (1940 TO PRESENT)

Saul Kripke is one of the most famous philosophers of the late 20th and early 21st centuries. He was educated at Harvard, taking an undergraduate degree in mathematics, then taught at Harvard, Rockefeller and Princeton universities. He currently teaches at CUNY Graduate Centre. Kripke has made signal contributions to many areas of philosophy and logic. As a teenager he made significant technical contributions to the study of modal logic. In philosophy he is best known for his two books: *Naming and Necessity* (1972 and 1980) and *Wittgenstein on Rules and Private Language* (1982). The first book had a revolutionary impact on the philosophy of language and resuscitated the study of metaphysics. Using his new linguistic framework, Kripke defended various essentialist theses about individuals and **natural kinds**, and criticized the mind–brain identity thesis. His second book revived interest in the later Wittgenstein's philosophy of language. Kripke argued that Wittgenstein advanced a sceptical paradox about meaning to which he (Wittgenstein) then proposed a sceptical solution. This solution implied that meaning is essentially public and that attributions of meaning are non-factual (neither true nor false). Some have complained that Kripke misinterprets Wittgenstein, but Kripke's contribution is significant in its own right.

● DO ORDINARY OBJECTS ENDURE OR PERDURE?

How we respond to these puzzles depends, in part, on how we conceive of ordinary objects, in our examples artefacts, and their identity over time. In recent years, two competing theories have emerged. According to one theory, ordinary objects persist by perduring. According to the alternative theory, such objects persist by enduring.

The perdurance theory

According to the perdurantist, ordinary objects are four-dimensional entities, with temporal parts as well as spatial ones. A spatio-temporal object persists through time by having different temporal parts (suitably related to each other) at different times. These temporal parts may themselves be composed of temporal parts or else composed of instantaneous three-dimensional slices.

The perdurantist view of ordinary objects is analogous to the standard view of events and processes. An event, such as my last birthday party, is a four-dimensional entity of, e.g., four hours duration. It is composed of four hour-long temporal parts, which are themselves composed of temporal parts. The party itself does not wholly exist at any one time during that four hours – only a part of it exists then. We would not say, without qualification, that the party was both quiet and raucous. We would say that it had an initial temporal part (the first hour) which was quiet, and a later temporal part (the last hour) which was raucous. The party exists in virtue of the existence of its various temporal parts.

A spatial analogy can illuminate the perdurantist view. The Hume Highway runs from Melbourne to Sydney. One stretch of the highway runs from Canberra to the glorious city of Goulburn. But the Hume Highway does not wholly exist in its Canberra–Goulburn segment, only a part of it exists there. The highway is composed of all its various spatial segments. For the perdurantist, this is analogous to the persistence of an ordinary object through time. An ordinary object persists by having different temporal parts at different times. Moreover, just as two roads may share a common spatial segment, so two four-dimensional objects may share a common temporal part (as we shall see presently).

I call this view 'perdurantism' rather than 'four-dimensionalism' since the doctrine would apply to temporal objects lacking any spatial dimensions (e.g., immaterial souls). Such objects are not four-dimensional.

The endurantist view

On the endurantist view, ordinary objects have no temporal parts and are 'wholly present' at all times at which they exist. You exist wholly today, and you existed wholly yesterday, and you will (hopefully) exist wholly tomorrow. You today are literally identical to yourself yesterday; a single three-dimensional object has endured. (In contrast, for the perdurantist, today's temporal part and yesterday's temporal part are numerically distinct parts which, along with your other temporal parts, compose you.)

I call this view 'endurantism' rather than 'three-dimensionalism' since the doctrine would apply to extensionless points in space. Such objects are not three-dimensional.

Preliminary comments on perdurantism vs endurantism

(i) It is sometimes said that perdurantism is an inevitable consequence of the B theory of time, and endurantism an inevitable consequence of the A theory. (See Chapter 8.) So any argument for the B theory of time would be an argument for perdurantism. But this is not the case.

The A theory/B theory dispute concerns the nature of time; the perdurantist/ endurantist dispute concerns the nature of ordinary objects. There is no inconsistency in being a B theorist and an endurantist, or in being an A theorist and a perdurantist. Admittedly, it is common for B theorists to be perdurantists (David Lewis is the obvious example), and common for A theorists to be endurantists (e.g., A.N. Prior), but there is no logical inevitability to these positions.

(ii) There is no argument from modern physics to perdurantism. Since the world would exhibit the same appearances and causal features whichever theory was true, there cannot be any such argument. The debate between pedurantism and endurantism is a philosophical one.

(iii) It has often been claimed that the endurantist, unlike the perdurantist, can give no consistent account of change. Suppose that Fred is fat but was thin. If Fred is wholly present when fat, and was wholly present when he was thin, then Fred is both fat and thin, which is a contradiction. The perdurantist is committed to no such contradiction since it is not the same object which is both fat and thin. Rather an earlier temporal part of Fred (Fred-at-t0) is thin, while a different temporal part of Fred (Fred-at-t1) is fat. For the perdurantist, change consists in different temporal parts of a single four-dimensional object having incompatible properties.

However, it is an illusion to think that endurantists cannot give a consistent account of change. They have at least two options. If they incline towards the A theory of time, they can insist on the tenses being taken seriously. It is misleading to say 'Fred is fat and thin'. Rather, Fred is fat and was thin. But this is not a contradiction. If they incline towards the B theory, they could relativize properties to times. Thus Fred is fat-at-t1 and thin-at-t0. Again there is no contradiction. Moreover, the endurantist's relativization of properties to times is hardly more objectionable than the perdurantist's relativization of objects to times (e.g., Fred-at-t1).

One way to decide between perdurantism and endurantism, if the matter can be decided, is by seeing how each theory deals with the puzzles of the previous section.

ENDURANCE AND PERDURANCE

How should we conceive of ordinary objects, such as you and me, horses and oak trees, statues and ships? Are these objects three-dimensional, 'wholly present' at every time at which they exist? Or are they four-dimensional, spread out in space-time, composed of temporal parts as much as spatial ones? The endurantist thinks that ordinary objects are three-dimensional; the perdurantist that they are four-dimensional. The perdurantist's account of cases of spatial coincidence is the more plausible. However, both theories have problems describing coherently the Ship of Theseus story, in which the continuously repaired ship and the re-constituted ship are both candidates to be Theseus's ship.

• THE THREE PUZZLES EXAMINED

The perdurantist and endurantist will treat differently of our puzzles. The cases of David and Lump, and of Lumpl and Goliath, seem to commit us to the apparently unacceptable consequence of numerically distinct objects occupying the same space at the same time (in virtue of being composed of the very same matter at that time). The challenge is to show either that there is no such consequence or that the consequence is not as absurd as it at first seems.

Those who follow John Locke will take the second option. On Locke's view, exact coincidence of numerically distinct objects is not, in itself, an absurdity. What is absurd is only the idea that two things of the same kind (two statues, two people, etc.) might occupy exactly the same space at the same time. As Locke writes: 'whatever exists anywhere at any time, excludes *all of the same kind*, and is there itself alone.'[3] So we have Locke's Principle:

> (LP) If x and y are numerically distinct objects of the same kind, they cannot occupy exactly the same space at the same time.

Given (LP), there is no absurdity in David and Lump, or in Goliath and Lumpl, occupying the same space at the same time since David and Goliath are statues, while Lump and Lumpl are lumps. Statues and lumps are different kinds of thing, with different **criteria of identity**. According to (LP), statues exclude other statues from occupying exactly the same space, but they don't exclude other kinds of object.

However, some will think (LP) overly concessive. Standard mereology (the logic of part and whole) maintains the following extensionality principle:

> (EP) If x and y are objects with the same (proper) parts, then x = y.

The import of this principle will depend on whether we accept perdurantism or endurantism, but clearly it is a stricter principle than Locke's. (EP) makes no exception for cases where x and y are of different kinds. (EP) is a clear and intuitive principle, typically endorsed by perdurantists. Whether it is ultimately acceptable remains to be seen.

David and Lump

The name 'Lump' was introduced on Monday and refers to a particular lump of clay. The name 'David' was introduced on Friday, and refers to a statue. On Friday, David and Lump occupy exactly the same space and are composed of the very same molecules.

All parties must agree that Lump ≠ David. Lump existed before David, so obviously they cannot be identical. This non-identity is consistent with (LP) since David and Lump are not objects of the same kind (David is a statue, Lump is a lump of clay).

What does (EP) imply about this case? Now it does matter whether we accept perdurantism or endurantism. If we are perdurantists, the non-identity of David and Lump is consistent with (EP) since David and Lump do not share all proper parts (e.g., Lump's Monday part is not a part of David). Of course, once David exists, David and Lump then share a temporal segment. For example, the Friday to Sunday temporal part of David is (identical to) the Friday to Sunday temporal part of Lump.

If we are endurantists we must reject (EP). If David and Lump are three-dimensional objects with no temporal parts, then David and Lump are both wholly present on Friday. On Friday they have all and only the same proper parts. Hence, by (EP), David = Lump. So endurantism, the verdict that David ≠ Lump, and (EP), form an inconsistent triad. Since all agree that David ≠ Lump, the endurantist must reject (EP).

Lumpl and Goliath

Though superficially similar, the case of Lumpl and Goliath is significantly different from the David and Lump case. It is designed so that Lumpl and Goliath share all their historical and spatio-temporal properties. They come into existence at the same time, they go out of existence at the same time, and they are at all times composed of the very same molecules. Should we therefore hold that Lumpl = Goliath?

A defender of nothing stronger than (LP) can allow that Lumpl ≠ Goliath. (LP) does not prohibit complete spatio-temporal coincidence of distinct objects, provided the objects are of different kinds. Since Lumpl is a lump and Goliath is a statue, they are of different kinds.

The endurantist response

Since they share all and only the same proper parts (EP) implies that Lumpl = Goliath. The endurantist, however, cannot accept this verdict, and should regard the Lumpl/Goliath example simply as an extension of the David/Lump example.

If David and Lump can both be wholly present yet numerically distinct, the same should be said of Lumpl and Goliath. It would be odd to hold that two wholly present objects can coincide for some of the time, but impossible to coincide at all times. Indeed, the endurantist would hold that had David and Lump coincided exactly at all times, they would still have been distinct. (As Kripke has reminded us, distinct objects are necessarily distinct.[4]) But that imaginary scenario is just the scenario of Lumpl and Goliath. The endurantist must (once again) reject (EP) and hold that Lumpl and Goliath are numerically distinct.

The perdurantist response

The perdurantist accepts (EP) since it provides a **criterion of identity** for four-dimensional objects: A and B are identical just if they share all and only the same (spatial and temporal) parts. Hence the perdurantist must hold that Lumpl = Goliath. But now we encounter a problem mentioned above: Lumpl and Goliath appear to differ in their modal properties. Goliath has the modal property of being essentially statue-shaped, but Lumpl lacks that property. Lumpl could have been squeezed into a ball and still existed; not so with Goliath. But if Lumpl and Goliath fail to share all properties then, by Leibniz's Law, they cannot be identical.

The perdurantist has a problem. Two principles perdurantists regard as constitutive of identity ((EP) and Leibniz's Law) yield – or appear to yield – incompatible verdicts in the Lumpl/Goliath case. One well-known perdurantist, David Lewis, claims that appearances are deceptive.[5] Lewis holds that Lumpl = Goliath, but that this involves no violation of Leibniz's Law.

We think that Lumpl ≠ Goliath because we are impressed by an argument such as the following:

1 Goliath is essentially statue-shaped;
2 Lumpl is not essentially statue-shaped; so
3 Lumpl ≠ Goliath.

Lewis thinks that this argument is invalid. Recall Lewis's counterpart-theoretic semantics (see Chapter 4). Lewis rejects transworld identity in favour of similarity relations between world-bound individuals. An object A is essentially F just if all A's counterparts (other-worldly entities similar to A in relevant respects) are F. But there are a range of counterpart relations, and which relation a modal predicate picks out depends on how the object in question is named or described. An object may have one set of counterparts when named or described in one way, and a different set when named or described in another way.

Since 'Goliath' is the name of a statue, (1) attributes to Goliath the property of being such that all of its statue-counterparts are statue-shaped. Since 'Lumpl' names a piece of clay, the property (2) denies of Lumpl is that of being such that all of its piece-of-clay counterparts are statue-shaped. These are different properties: the property attributed to Goliath is not the property denied to Lumpl. Consequently, we can hold that (1) and (2) are true, but (3) false, consistently with Leibniz's Law.

In contravention of Kripke's thesis of the necessity of identity, Lewis holds that 'Lumpl = Goliath' is true, but **contingent**. Lumpl is Goliath in our imagined world w, but in other possible worlds Lumpl is not Goliath (e.g., a world w* in which Lumpl and Goliath come into existence simultaneously, but Lumpl is later squeezed into a ball). But the contingent identity in w of 'Lumpl = Goliath' does not violate Leibniz's Law. There is no modal property which Goliath has but Lumpl lacks – for the reason given above.

Note that Lewis can make the very same response to a natural objection to perdurantism: (i) I might have died at the age 30; (ii) no four-dimensional entity could have had a temporal extent different from its actual extent; so (iii) I am not a four-dimensional entity. Lewis can concede both premises, but argue, as above, that the conclusion does not follow.

Lewis's solution is certainly ingenious; but, since there are objections to counterpart theory, it is also controversial. (See Chapter 4.)

SHIP OF THESEUS

The voyages of the Ship of Theseus illustrate many of the possibilities and para-doxes of identity over time. One story illustrates that a ship can survive complete dismantlement and re-assembly. Another story illustrates the possibility of a ship surviving a total replacement of its parts. We can combine these two stories and imagine that Theseus's ship is continuously repaired, but each removed plank is retained and later used to construct an exact replica of Theseus's original ship. The deep question raised here is not 'which of the two later ships is Theseus's ship?' (to which there is no objective answer). The real puzzle is that whichever ship we deem to be Theseus's ship, seriously unintuitive conse-quences follow. This is true whether we are endurantists or perdurantists.

The Ship of Theseus

Of the three scenarios involving the Ship of Theseus, neither (a) nor (b) is puzzling or paradoxical. But they do illustrate two extreme possibilities. Scenario (a) illustrates the possibility that artefacts can exist intermittently. Since – plausibly – no ship exists between dismantlement and reassembly, Theseus's ship first exists, then goes out of existence, then comes back into existence. It is the same ship since constructed out of the same planks according to the same plan. This is unusual but not paradoxical.

Scenario (b) illustrates the possibility that an artefact such as a ship can survive a complete replacement of its parts. As long as the exchange of planks occurs in the normal working life in the ship, we have no hesitation in judging the later ship to be identical to the earlier one. A total exchange of matter is also a feature of many living organisms, such as the human body. Identity over time is not imperilled by such a circumstance.

But a truly puzzling scenario arises when we combine (a) and (b), which is effectively what (c) does. In (a) and (b) there is only one later candidate to be Theseus's ship, but in (c) there are two candidates, the continuously repaired ship (call it X) and the re-constituted ship (call it Y), both of whom have a claim to be the Ship of Theseus. Which ship has the stronger claim?

(In Figure 5.1, 'Y1' refers to the re-constituted ship in (a); 'X1' refers to the continu-ously repaired ship in (b); 'X' refers to the continuously repaired ship in (c); and 'Y' refers to the re-constituted ship in (c).)

This question cannot receive a straight answer. If our interest is in working ships, considered as transporters of men and goods, then we might opt for X. If we are anti-quarians, looking to make a purchase for a museum, we might opt for Y. Either option is defensible. Yet either option has an odd consequence. (This odd conse-quence would ensue even if we thought it vague or indeterminate which of the two later ships is the Ship of Theseus.)

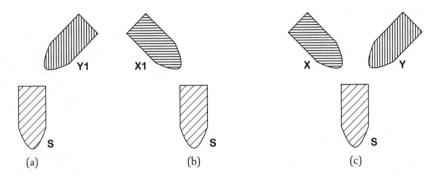

Figure 5.1

Suppose we say that Theseus's ship (S) in (c) is X and not Y. (An analogous problem will arise if we were to judge that S is Y but not X.) Can we not now say: although S ≠ Y, had the removed planks not been replaced (so that there was no continuously repaired ship), S would have been identical to Y (as in (a))? (This question assumes that Y = Y1.) For this scenario is just (a), and we agreed that the re-constituted ship there is Theseus's ship. But this result violates Kripke's well-established doctrine of the necessity of identity and non-identity. According to that doctrine, since 'S' and 'Y' are both proper names, if S ≠ Y, then necessarily S ≠ Y.

In other words, the common sense assumption that Y = Y1, together with the judgements that S = Y1 and S ≠ Y, conflict with Kripke's thesis of the necessity of identity.

THE NECESSITY OF IDENTITY

It is a plausible theorem in standard modal logic that (x) (y) (if x = y, necessarily x = y). By Leibniz's Law, if x = y, they share all properties. x has the property of being necessarily identical to x. If x = y, y must have that property too. Hence: if x = y, necessarily x = y. (Equally plausible is the theorem that (x) (y) (if x ≠ y, necessarily x ≠ y).) Saul Kripke argued that certain terms in natural language (in particular, proper names and natural kind terms) are **rigid designators** (i.e., they do not shift referents across possible situations). Kripke held that identity statements containing only rigid designators are, if true, necessarily true. Thus, despite being empirical discoveries, 'Tully = Cicero' and 'Hesperus = Phosphorus' are necessary truths. Note that Kripke's thesis does not follow from the modal theorems. The modal theorems are consistent with the non-rigidity of proper names; they imply nothing about proper names in natural languages. Some have thought that there are contingent identity sentences (containing only proper names), contrary to Kripke's thesis. See the discussion of Lumpl and Goliath in the text.

The endurantist response

To respect the necessity of identity and non-identity, the endurantist must deny that Y = Y1, even though both ships are constructed out of the very same planks according to the same plan. However, if Y ≠ Y1, we have the following odd consequence. Someone in (c) could point to Y and say 'Had the removed planks not been replaced, this ship (Y) would not have existed.' The ship constructed out of those planks would then have been Y1, and Y ≠ Y1. That is, whether Y or Y1 exists depends on whether, elsewhere, removed planks are or are not replaced. This is strange because we don't think that the existence of a particular ship (or of anything else in space and time) depends on what happens in a region of the universe which exerts no causal influence on it.

The perdurantist response

Perdurantists can avoid this consequence. A perdurantist who rejects the necessity of identity could concede that Y = Y1 and hold that S and Y are distinct ships in (c), but identical in (a) (since Y1 is Y). However, it's not clear how this is to be motivated. The contingent identity of Lumpl with Goliath was rendered consistent with Leibniz's Law by virtue of Lumpl and Goliath being different kinds of thing, and hence generating different counterpart relations. But S and Y are things of the same kind (*viz.*, ships).

Conceding this point, the standard perdurantist response is to regard (c) as the superposition of (a) and (b). That is, the perdurantist regards (c) as involving only two ships (X and Y) which share a common pre-repair temporal segment. Prior to any removal of planks, the continuously repaired ship and the re-constituted ship existed and shared a temporal segment. X is the ship which exists throughout in (b); Y is the ship which exists throughout in (a), and X is not the same ship as Y. But both ships exist in (c), sharing a common early stage. See Figure 5.2.

The advantage of this view is that the odd consequences of endurantism are avoided. The continuously repaired ship in (c) is the continuously repaired ship in (b), and the re-constituted ship in (c) is the re-constituted ship in (a). So we could not point to the re-constituted ship in (c) (Y) and truly say 'Had the removed planks not been

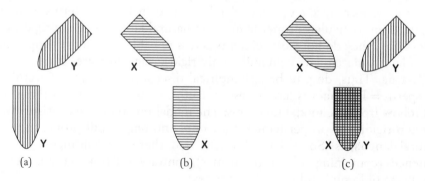

(a)　　　　　　　(b)　　　　　　　(c)

Figure 5.2

replaced, this ship would not have existed'. The very same re-constituted ship (Y) exists (in (a) and (c)) whether or not the continuously repaired ship (X) exists. Its existence does not depend on whether replacements are made elsewhere.

The disadvantage of the perdurantist view is that we can no longer think of (a) – (c) as three possible futures for one and the same ship. For the ship in (a) is distinct from the ship in (b) (X ≠ Y) and (c) contains them both (each sharing a common pre-repair stage). But this is counter-intuitive. Surely those present at the construction of the Ship of Theseus could sensibly wonder whether the future for *that* ship will be like (a) or (b) or (c). Yet the perdurantist must deny this.

There is another problem for perdurantism. In scenario (c), the name 'Ship of Theseus', when originally introduced, has no clear reference. Unbeknownst to those present at the naming ceremony, they are staring at a temporal part shared by two overlapping ships. To which ship does 'this ship' in 'I name this ship the Ship of Theseus' refer to? If I say 'this ship will survive complete replacement of its planks' is what I say true, false or neither?

• CONCLUDING REMARKS

The main aims of this chapter were to display and examine the various puzzles surrounding identity and constitution, to introduce the different theories of the perdurantist and endurantist, and to see how these theories cope with the puzzle cases.

In both statue examples, the perdurantist response is the more palatable. The endurantist must reject the intuitive principle (EP), and must hold that two numerically distinct but wholly present objects can be spatially coincident at one time or even throughout their entire histories. This is strange. However, in the case of the Ship of Theseus there are serious problems with both the endurantist and perdurantist responses.

• STUDY QUESTIONS

- Can you think of any counterexamples to Locke's Principle?
- How should we distinguish endurantism from perdurantism?
- Could the extensionality principle (EP) ever be given up?
- How plausible is David Lewis's solution to the Lumpl/Goliath conundrum?
- How should we describe the scenario where two later ships compete for the title of 'Ship of Theseus'?

• ANNOTATED FURTHER READING

A. Gibbard, 'Contingent Identity', *Journal of Philosophical Logic*, 4 (1975), pp. 187–221. A classic paper which introduces and attempts to resolve the puzzle of Lumpl and Goliath.

P. van Inwagen, *Material Beings* (Ithaca: Cornell University Press, 1990). Van Inwagen argues that there are no complex material objects, hence no statues or ships (only simples arranged statue- and ship-wise). Ingenious if not compelling.

P. van Inwagen, 'Temporal Parts and Identity across Time', *Monist*, Vol. 83, No.3 (2000), pp. 437–59. Very readable critique of perdurantism by one of its stoutest critics.

D. Lewis, 'Counterparts of Persons and Their Bodies', *Journal of Philosophy*, Vol. 68, No.7 (1971), pp. 203–11. A brilliant attempt to accommodate all our intuitions about the Lumpl/Goliath and related cases.

S. Kripke, *Naming and Necessity* (Oxford: Blackwell, 1980). One of the most important books in recent metaphysics and the philosophy of language. A sustained defence of the necessity of identity sentences containing only proper names.

D. Wiggins, *Sameness and Substance* (Oxford: Blackwell, 1980) and *Sameness and Substance Renewed* (Cambridge: Cambridge University Press, 2001). Masterful discussion of issues to do with identity, self and the world.

• INTERNET RESOURCES

Katherine Hawley, 'Temporal Parts', *The Stanford Encyclopedia of Philosophy* (Fall 2008 Edition), ed. Edward N. Zalta, URL = <http://plato.stanford.edu/archives/fall2008/entries/temporal-parts/>.

Harold Noonan, 'Identity', *The Stanford Encyclopedia of Philosophy (Winter 2009 Edition)*, ed. Edward N. Zalta, URL = <http://plato.stanford.edu/archives/win2009/entries/identity/>.

Ryan Wasserman, 'Material Constitution', *The Stanford Encyclopedia of Philosophy* (Spring 2009 Edition), ed. Edward N. Zalta, URL = <http://plato.stanford.edu/archives/spr2009/entries/material-constitution/>.

• NOTES

1. A. Gibbard, 'Contingent Identity', *Journal of Philosophical Logic*, 4 (1975), pp. 187–221. Note that although Gibbard holds that Lumpl is Goliath, and contingently so, he is not a counterpart theorist.
2. Plutarch, *Lives*, 22–3.
3. J. Locke, *Essay Concerning Human Understanding*, ed. W. Carroll (Bristol: Thoemmes, 1990), II, 28.1.
4. See S. Kripke, *Naming and Necessity* (Oxford: Blackwell, 1980).
5. See, e.g., 'Counterparts of Persons and Their Bodies', *Journal of Philosophy*, Vol. 68, No. 7 (1971), pp. 203–11.

6

objects and properties

• INTRODUCTION

What are objects and properties, and how are they connected? Are objects just bundles of properties or are they **substances** in which properties **inhere**? Are properties universals, identical in their instances, or can we explain what it is for an object to have a property without appeal to universals? These are among the most venerable questions in metaphysics, dating back to the ancient Greeks, Plato and Aristotle.

Philosophers who hold that we must appeal to universals in order to explain the nature of properties and relations are traditionally called 'realists'; those who deny this are traditionally called 'nominalists'. But there are varieties of each position: realism has Platonic, Aristotelian and Russellian versions; nominalism divides into predicate nominalism, class nominalism, resemblance nominalism and trope theory.

One important difference between these versions of realism and nominalism concerns their conception of objects. Greek realists hold that objects or particulars are individual substances distinct from the universals which inhere in them. On this dualist view, objects and properties constitute two quite different categories of being. Later realists, such as Bertrand Russell, and some nominalists, such as the trope theorist D.C. Williams, regard objects as bundles of properties (though they understand properties quite differently).

Historically, nominalists have been opposed to **abstract** entities (existing outside space and time). However, nominalism, as I am using the term here, is just the denial of the view that properties are universals. So understood, nominalism is compatible with the existence of abstract objects such as numbers and sets.

PLATO (427–347 BC)

The founder of Western philosophy, Plato was born into an aristocratic family in Athens, and became a follower of Socrates. After Socrates death in 399 BC, Plato began to write Socratic dialogues in memory of his teacher. A number of years later Plato founded the Academy, the first university-style institution in the West, which provided sanctuary to leading mathematicians, scientists and philosophers. Plato's two central doctrines were his Theory of Forms and his theory of the immortality of the soul. In contrast to the ephemeral, changing world we see around us, the Forms are abstract and changeless, the true objects of knowledge. Thus the Form of Justice exists in an abstract realm, outside space and time. Individual human acts are just in virtue of 'participating' in the Form Justice. We all had knowledge of the Forms prior to our current physical incarnation. The Forms are the foundation of Plato's metaphysics, but also play a key role in his political philosophy. In Plato's ideal city (outlined in his most famous work, *The Republic*) it is the philosophers who rule since they alone understand the Forms, in particular the Form Good.

• UNIVERSALS

We should first note two different conceptions of universals: Platonic and Aristotelian. Ideal geometric shapes were the model for Plato's universals (or 'Forms' as he called them). The ideal triangle exists in an abstract realm outside space and time. So too Plato's Forms are abstract entities, which exist whether or not they have any **concrete** instances. The universal *octadecagon* exists, on the Platonic view, even if the concrete world contains no octadecagons.

Aristotle's model for universals was drawn from that of species in biology. Since a species cannot exist unless it has some members, so a universal cannot exist unless it has some instances. Aristotle's universals are therefore not abstract, but are located where their instances are located and nowhere else.

Despite these differences the essence of Greek realism is reasonably clear: objects ('particulars' or 'individual substances' in the more traditional vocabulary) have or instantiate properties; two (or more) objects can, quite literally, have one and the same property; hence properties are universals, which can be wholly present in two or more objects. Unlike particulars, universals are capable of multiple instantiation in more than one object (they are repeatable).

Two arguments for Greek realism

(i) The semantic argument

One motivation for Greek realism, and certainly one of Plato's motivations, stems from considerations to do with the meaning of **general terms**. Suppose we begin by assuming a referential theory of meaning, according to which the meaning of a word is the entity referred to by the word. In the case of **singular terms**, e.g., ordinary proper names such as 'Socrates', 'Red Rum' and 'Edinburgh' there is little difficulty identifying the entities which, according to the referential theory, are the meanings of these words: the man Socrates, the horse Red Rum and the city Edinburgh, respectively. But what of general terms such as 'horse' and 'city' (i.e., terms which apply to many entities)? What entities do these words refer to? They do not refer to one particular horse or to one particular city (for why that horse or that city?). Hence, thought Plato, if general terms don't name particulars, they must name universals (such as *cityhood* and *horseness*).

Few philosophers now accept this semantic argument for universals.

(a)   The argument assumes that, if 'horse' refers, it refers either to a particular horse or to the universal *horseness*. But there is a third possibility: the general term 'horse' refers to each individual horse. If such 'divided reference' occurs, the semantic argument is broken-backed.

(b)   Why should we accept the underlying assumption that the meaning of a word is some entity denoted by the word? Names such as 'Santa Claus' and 'Sherlock Holmes', for example, are perfectly meaningful, yet there is no object to which they refer (they are '**empty names**'). If meaning is not reference, general terms may be meaningful without referring to anything at all.

(ii) The metaphysical argument

However, there is another, metaphysical, argument for universals. It runs as follows:

> Consider two exactly similar red spheres. They have the same colour (amongst other similarities). That is, the colour of one sphere is literally the same as, i.e., **numerically identical** to, the colour of the other. What is present in one is also present in the other. In contrast, no particular (such as Red Rum) can be wholly present in two places at once. Of course, one part of Red Rum (e.g., its left front leg) can be, and will be, in a different place from another part (e.g., its right front leg). But the horse cannot be, in its entirety, in two places at once. In contrast, the essence of a universal is its repeatability: it can be wholly present in different objects at the same time. Thus, in order to explain the truism that different objects can have the same property, we must appeal to universals.

The problem with this argument is that not every use of 'same' expresses strict numerical identity. Some uses do: e.g., when we say of two children that they 'have the same mother'. In such a case, we really do mean that the mother of one child is literally, numerically, the same as the mother of the other. But consider the use of 'same' in 'he has the same smile as his father'. Here the word 'same' expresses **qualitative identity** (i.e., striking similarity), not numerical identity. The sense of 'same' in 'they have the same mother' is quite different from its sense in 'they have the same smile'. Consequently, a defender of the metaphysical argument has to show, without begging the question, that 'same' in 'the colour of this sphere is the same as the colour of that sphere' (and similar examples) expresses numerical rather than qualitative identity.

ARISTOTLE (384–322 BC)

Born in the Macedonian city of Stagira, Aristotle spent much of his later life in Athens. He enrolled in Plato's Academy in 367 BC, and remained there for 20 years, first as a student, then as a teacher and writer. He left Athens after Plato's death (347 BC) but later returned to set up his own school, the Lyceum. Aristotle was the most systematic philosopher of antiquity. He originated the conception of philosophy as an intellectual inquiry, divided up into distinct branches: logic, scientific inquiry (largely, biology and cosmology), metaphysics, the mind–body problem, ethics and politics, and literary criticism. Aristotle made original contributions to all these areas and, in doing so, helped to define what we now think of as philosophy. He was much discussed by the medievals after translations of his works into Latin appeared in the 12th century. His influence was further reinforced, and legitimated, when Aquinas made Aristotelianism the basis for Catholic theology.

Four objections to Greek realism

(i)   Some find the idea of a universal hard to understand. How can anything be 'wholly present' in different objects at the same time? We can distinguish two objections here:

    (a)   Simple disbelief that an entity could be 'wholly present' in different objects at the same time. But this is hardly a decisive objection. One familiar and intuitive conception of what it is for an object to persist through time relies on an analogous idea (that of a single object being 'wholly present' at different times). (See Chapter 5.)

    (b)   Objects are said to instantiate universals. But what is instantiation? What is it for an object to instantiate a universal? This question is especially pressing on the Platonic conception, where instantiation is said to hold between a concrete particular and an abstract universal. How can something in space and time instantiate something outside space and time?

(ii) Indeed, Plato's Forms seem to be objects or particulars not universals. The Form of Good, e.g., can be referred to using names and definite descriptions. But how can one particular (albeit abstract) inhere in other particulars? (Frege had a related problem.)

(iii) This last objection cannot be pressed against Aristotle, but a different objection presents itself: how are Aristotle's this-worldly universals, wholly present in their instances and nowhere else, different from scattered particulars? My copy of the *Encyclopedia Brittannica* is a scattered particular. It is a single concrete object yet it has discontinuous parts (some volumes are in the billiard room, some in the library). Why is the Aristotelian universal of (say) *greenness* not similarly a scattered particular, with discontinuous parts in different locations throughout the universe?

(iv) Finally, there is a problem for Greek realism concerning that which instantiates universals (the object, particular or individual substance). A substance (such as a particular horse) is not identical with its properties, but has or instantiates those properties. Is it supposed then that we can conceive of the horse apart from all its properties? Yet this seems impossible. Further, how is the horse itself knowable if all we perceive and respond to are its properties? Or, in perceiving the horse's colour, shape, etc., do we thereby perceive the horse?

• RUSSELL'S BUNDLE THEORY

Bertrand Russell (1872–1970) is a realist who rejects the substance/universal dualism of the Greeks and regards ordinary objects not as substances but as bundles of universals. He thus avoids the standard objections to Greek realism just rehearsed. For example, there can be no puzzle concerning the tie between substance and universal if there are no substances (as traditionally understood).

Russell was impressed by our final objection to Greek realism. An individual substance or particular, he wrote:

> cannot be defined or recognised or known; it is something serving the merely grammatical purpose of providing the subject in a subject–predicate sentence such as 'This is red'. And to allow grammar to dictate our metaphysics is now generally recognised to be dangerous. ... The notion of a substance as a peg on which to hang predicates is repugnant.[1]

Russell's response was to eliminate the category of substance and to conceive of ordinary objects as bundles of universals. Objects are like onions not avocados: there is no stone of substance within.

Having dispensed with substances, Russell needed some account of what unifies a single object and what distinguishes different objects. To explain the unity of a single object, he appealed to a notion of 'compresence', where (a) the qualities that make up an object, such as my chair, are compresent with each other, and (b) no other quality in the universe is compresent with all those qualities. These qualities, for Russell, are universals: e.g., the brownness in my carpet is strictly identical to the brownness in my desk.

Two objections to Russell's theory

(i) 'Compresence' is only a label. We are not told how various universals manage to combine, without inhering in a substance, to form a single object, such as a particular chair or horse. What unites the elements of the bundle so they comprise a single object?

(ii) What makes objects distinct from each other, on Russell's view? As Russell points out, although humans have some qualities in common (such as humanity), no two humans are exactly alike. There is always some difference between two individuals, however trivial (e.g., differences in the number of hairs on their heads, or in the number of molecules composing their left hands, etc.). As Russell says, '[i]t is only the assemblage of qualities that makes the instance unique.'[2]

Russell can claim that, whenever two individuals are distinct, there will be some difference in the corresponding bundles of universals in virtue of which they are distinct. (That is, clause (b) in his account of unity is enough to guarantee that distinct objects are counted as distinct.)

However, this claim merely invites the following objection. Even if no two actual objects are exactly alike, is it not possible for there to be two exactly similar objects? For example, could there not be a world containing only two exactly resembling spheres? Yet for Russell there cannot be such a world. If objects are bundles of universals, then identity of bundle implies identity of object (same bundle, same object). If the spheres are composed of the same universals, they cannot be numerically distinct. But, intuitively, it is possible for there to be a universe containing only two exactly similar spheres. Russell's theory rules out this possibility, and this is an objection to his theory.

It might be replied that the spheres can be distinguished by their respective locations. Sphere A occupies region R while sphere B occupies R*. Since A and B occupy different regions, A ≠ B. But this does not work. For regions, and the points that make them up, are objects too, and hence bundles of universals. How can Russell distinguish R from R*? Although we can say that R and R* are distinct regions, Russell cannot. R and R* are composed of the very same universals (e.g., both are occupied by a sphere, both are one meter from a sphere, etc.).

UNIVERSALS

Since Plato, many philosophers have held that properties and relations are universals, 'wholly present' in their instances. If my billiard ball is red, that is because redness (the universal) 'inheres' in the ball (the particular). Similarly, if any other ball is red that is because the very same universal 'inheres' in that ball too. If a red ball is one foot from a white ball that is because *being one foot* from (the universal) inheres in the spatial distance between them. Some relations (the so-called internal relations, such as *being taller than* or *being redder than*) are not fundamental. That Fred is taller than Bill is necessitated by the fact that, e.g., Fred is six foot tall and Bill is five foot tall. As long as we record the particular heights of Fred and Bill in the inventory of being, we do not need to add that Fred is taller than Bill. In contrast, external relations, such as *being to the left of* or *being one foot apart*, are not necessitated by their terms, and are genuine additions to being.

• VARIETIES OF NOMINALISM

We have seen that there are problems facing Greek and Russellian realism. Are the prospects for nominalism any brighter? Let us examine the range of views that attempt to account for objects and their properties without appeal to universals.

Predicate nominalism

According to predicate nominalism, for x to have the property of F-ness is for the predicate 'F' to apply to, or be true of, x. A sphere is red because the predicate 'red' applies to it.

This theory is open to the following two objections:

(i)   There are surely properties in the universe for which there will never exist any natural language predicate. Predicate nominalism seems constitutionally incapable of acknowledging the existence of such unknown properties.

(ii)   Predicate nominalism seems to put the cart before the horse. Intuitively, it's not that this sphere is red because 'red' applies to it; rather, 'red' applies to the sphere because it is red. (These objections also apply to concept nominalism: the view that x is F in virtue of the fact that x falls under the concept of F.)

Class nominalism

According to class nominalism, properties are sets or classes of objects. A sphere is red because it is a member of the class of red things.

Class nominalism avoids the first objection to predicate nominalism. Whether an object is a member of a certain class does not depend on whether we have discovered the class or have a word for it. (The class of electrons existed before we knew of it.) However, the second objection still seems to apply: intuitively our sphere is a member of the class of red things because it is red, not vice versa.

In addition, class nominalism incurs two objections of its own:

(i)   The relation of class membership is itself a universal, instantiated whenever an object is a member of a class. Hence, class nominalism is implicitly committed to universals, and so fails to be a genuine version of nominalism.

(ii) Suppose that all and only red things were round. In such a circumstance, the class of red things is the class of round things. According to class nominalism, the property of being red would then be the same as the property of being round – an absurd result.

Resemblance nominalism

According to resemblance nominalism, properties are classes of resembling objects. A sphere is red because it is a member of a class of resembling objects, where 'resemblance' is treated as a primitive, unanalysable relation.

However, there are three problems with this version of nominalism:

(i)   An object such as a red sphere is a member of a number of resembling classes. For example, it is a member of the class of red things and a member of the class of spherical things. Yet, clearly, the sphere is not red in virtue of resembling spherical things; it is red in virtue of resembling red things. That is, it is red because it resembles other objects in respect of colour (rather than shape). In which case resemblance is not an unanalysable relation, but admits of respects. Moreover, what are respects if not universals?

(ii) Russell had a similar objection: the relation of resemblance is itself a universal. He wrote:

> If we wish to avoid the universals whiteness and triangularity, we shall choose some particular patch of white or some particular triangle, and say that anything is white or a triangle if it has the right sort of resemblance to our chosen particular. But then the resemblance required will have to be a universal. Since there are many white things, the resemblance must hold between many pairs of particular white things; and this is the characteristic of a universal.[3]

In which case, as with class nominalism, resemblance nominalism has not avoided an implicit commitment to universals.

(iii) Finally, there is the problem of lonely objects. According to resemblance nominalism, an object is spherical just if it resembles other objects in respect of shape. But this rules out the possibility of a universe containing only one sphere.[4] This is surely an unpalatable consequence.

TROPES

Trope theory, though a minority view today, has been popular at various times throughout the history of philosophy, especially among medieval philosophers. Like all versions of nominalism, trope theory denies the existence of universals. In addition, trope theory holds that properties and relations are themselves particulars – 'abstract' particulars. ('Abstract' in the sense of fine, partial and diffuse, not in the sense of outside space and time.) Thus the redness of a particular billiard ball is an abstract particular, located where the ball is and nowhere else. A different but exactly resembling billiard ball has a numerically different but exactly resembling redness trope. There is no colour property common to, or instantiated in, both balls. Similarly with all other properties and relations. On a standard version of trope theory, ordinary particulars (i.e., what all theories classify as particulars – you, me, the next winner of the Melbourne Cup, etc.) are composed of abstract particulars. A billiard ball is composed of a colour trope, a shape trope, a weight trope, etc. The universe consists of tropes. They are the 'alphabet of being' out of which all else is constructed. Questions remain for trope theory. Could a colour trope exist all by itself? If not, why not? What binds tropes together to form single objects? Which tropes are basic or fundamental and which reducible or eliminable?

• TROPES

Trope theory is the most interesting and most extreme version of nominalism. Properties and relations are conceived of as (unrepeatable) particulars, called 'tropes'. Tropes are also called 'abstract particulars' – not because they are outside space and time, but because they are 'fine', 'subtle', 'partial' and 'diffuse'. Your weight, the colour of my eyes and the height of the Eiffel Tower are abstract particulars. Ordinary spatio-temporal objects, such as cars, trees and tigers, are concrete particulars, composed of abstract particulars or tropes. Events and facts are also held to be constructed out of tropes.

Suppose we have two red billiard balls before us. They are both red, but not because they share a common property. Rather, the redness of one ball is an (unrepeatable) particular, numerically distinct from, but exactly resembling, the redness of the other ball. In virtue of so resembling, we call them both 'red', but each redness is a distinct abstract particular or trope. Tropes are not just the elements of being, they are also the immediate objects of perception.

Defended by the medievals, and by G.F. Stout in the 19th century, trope theory was substantially developed by Donald Williams and Keith Campbell in the 20th century. For Williams, tropes are the fundamental entities, the 'alphabet of being', and resemblance and spatio-temporal distance are the fundamental relations between tropes. Two exactly resembling redness tropes are distinct in virtue of occupying different locations; the colour and shape tropes of a sphere are distinct in virtue of not resembling each other.

Ordinary concrete objects, such as cars, have parts, such as wheels and doors, which are themselves concrete particulars. But all concrete particulars are bundles of tropes. Williams' theory is thus the nominalistic counterpart of Russell's realist bundle theory. Both theories reject the category of substance, as traditionally conceived.

Motivation for trope theory

The great merit of trope theory is that it avoids all the objections canvassed so far. None of the objections to Greek realism apply. The relation between an ordinary object and its tropes is that of whole to part. The mysterious 'is' of instantiation is replaced by the more perspicuous 'is' of 'is a part of'. A sphere is red, not because the sphere instantiates the universal *redness*, but because a redness trope is a part of the bundle of tropes that is the sphere. No entities are said to be wholly present in different objects at the same time, no entities (abstract or concrete) are instantiated in other entities.

Trope theory also escapes the objections to other versions of nominalism because it doesn't analyse what it is for an object to have a property in terms of any relation between that object and something else (predicates, classes, resembling objects, etc.). If a sphere is red that is because it contains a red trope, and this is not a matter of the sphere standing in any relation to anything else.

Although trope theory helps itself to the notion of similarity or resemblance, it does not conceive of this relation, or any other relation, as a universal. A's resembling B and C's resembling D are distinct resemblance tropes, not a doubly instantiated universal. Finally, unlike Russell's bundle theory, trope theory has no problem acknowledging a possible world with two exactly resembling red spheres. The spheres are distinct in virtue of being composed of distinct, but exactly resembling, tropes.

Three problems for trope theory

(i)   Trope theorists replace instantiation with the part–whole relation. Ordinary objects are bundles of tropes, and an object is red if it contains a redness trope as a part. But can this view accommodate the plausible thought that some of an object's properties are essential to it? (See Chapter 4.) If Bill is essentially human, then the bundle that is Bill essentially contains a humanity trope as a part. But how can a bundle have essential parts? What could make a trope essential to a bundle?

(ii) Even if there is no problem of instantiation for the trope theorist, there is the problem of what binds tropes together to form a single object. (Russell, of course, had an analogous problem.) A bundle of tropes may be 'co-located' or 'compresent', but what is the glue that unifies them so that they constitute a single object? What are the structural relations between tropes? Why is it true, e.g., that anything with a size trope must have a shape trope? Are some tropes fundamental and others derivative or eliminable? More needs to be said.

(iii) The strategy of the trope theorist is to understand ordinary predication in terms of the part–whole relation. This works well enough in the case of predications involving concrete particulars, but what about predications involving tropes themselves? We can truly say many things of a given redness trope: it is red, coloured, red or green, my favourite trope, in Canberra, persisted through 2012, etc. Since a trope is not a bundle, we cannot regard 'this trope is red' as made true by a bundle's containing a redness trope. How then are we to understand such predications, other than in terms of the instantiation of a universal in a trope?

There are problems for trope theory, as there are for all other theories. Nonetheless, it is a novel account of the nature of objects and properties, and well worth further research.

• CONCLUDING REMARKS

We have covered a lot of difficult ground in this chapter and our conclusions are the following. There are problems facing both Greek and Russellian realism and problems facing nominalist accounts, both moderate and extreme. Trope theory may be a promising account of objects and properties, but that project still has much in the way of unfinished business. There is no problem-free theory of the tie between an object and its properties.

• STUDY QUESTIONS

- What is the difference between Platonic and Aristotelian conceptions of universals?
- What is the distinction between numerical and qualitative identity?
- Are there good objections to Russell's bundle theory?
- Is any version of nominalism defensible?
- What is a trope?

• ANNOTATED FURTHER READING

D.M. Armstrong, *Universals: An Opinionated Introduction* (Boulder: Westview Press, 1989). By far the best introduction to universals, written by one of their stoutest defenders.

K. Campbell, *Abstract Particulars* (Oxford: Basil Blackwell, 1990). A clear and trenchant defence of tropes. Utterly no-nonsense.

B. Russell, *The Problems of Philosophy* (Oxford: Oxford University Press, 1978). Written in 1912, this book remains one of the classic introductions to philosophy. In it Russell argues for the existence of universals and offers a famous objection to resemblance nominalism.

D.C. Williams, 'The Elements of Being', *Review of Metaphysics*, 7 (1953), pp. 3–18 and 171–92. A very readable, wonderfully informed, if idiosyncratic, elaboration of the project of 'analytic ontology' and its terminology, together with a defence of tropes as the building blocks of all that is.

• INTERNET RESOURCES

J. Bacon, 'Tropes', *The Stanford Encyclopedia of Philosophy* (Fall 2010 Edition), ed. Edward N. Zalta, forthcoming URL = <http://plato.stanford.edu/archives/fall2010/entries/tropes/>.

J.C. Bigelow (1998), 'Universals', *Routledge Encyclopedia of Philosophy*, ed. E. Craig. Retrieved 31 May 2006 from <http://www.rep.routledge.com/article/N065>.

C. Daly (2005), 'Properties', *Routledge Encyclopedia of Philosophy*, ed. E. Craig. Retrieved 31 May 2006 from <http://www.rep.routledge.com/article/N121SECT4>.

J. Schaffer 'The Individuation of Tropes', *Australasian Journal of Philosophy*, Vol. 79, No. 2 (2001) http://rsss.anu.edu.au/~schaffer/papers/Tropes.pdf.

C. Swoyer, 'Properties', *The Stanford Encyclopedia of Philosophy* (Winter 2000 edition), ed. Edward N. Zalta. Retrieved 31 May 2006 from <http://plato.stanford.edu/archives/win2000/entries/properties>.

• NOTES

1. B. Russell, *Human Knowledge, its Scope and Limits* (New York: Simon & Schuster, 1948). Reprinted in *Metaphysics: The Big Questions*, ed. P. Van Inwagen and D. Zimmerman (Oxford: Basil Blackwell, 1999), p. 54.
2. *Ibid.*, p. 57.
3. B. Russell, *The Problems of Philosophy* (Oxford: Oxford University Press, 1978), p. 55.
4. The modal realist is not vulnerable to this objection, nor to objection (ii) to class nominalism, since classes are not restricted to objects in just one possible world. (See Chapter 4.)

7

causation

• INTRODUCTION

Our language abounds with causal talk. We often use the word 'cause' itself –
'smoking causes cancer', 'her words caused offence', etc. – but we also use many
verbs which presuppose causation: 'they had to push their car', 'she pulled him
towards her', etc. Such talk raises a host of different questions, about which there is
little consensus.

The biggest question of all concerns the nature of causation itself. What is the relation
of causation? Is the causal reducible to the non-causal? Modern discussion of this
question was inaugurated by David Hume (1711–1776), who is one of the leading
advocates of the **reductionist** school. We examine Hume's theory, together with the
theory of a contemporary reductionist about causation, David Lewis. We also consider
an alternative view proposed by Elizabeth Anscombe. Finally, we consider whether
there is good reason to think backwards causation impossible.

Our concern is with singular causal claims (such as 'Sally shot Mary') and not with
general claims (such as 'HIV causes AIDS'). When we say 'A caused B' what kinds of
thing are A and B? If we go by the linguistic evidence, the answer is: various. We say
such things as:

(i)   The car killed the man.
(ii) The man died because the car hit him.
(iii) The impact of the car caused the man's death.

Each of these causal claims relate quite different kinds of entity. In (i) objects stand in
a causal relation, in (ii) facts, and in (iii) events. Are the related entities indeed
various, or should causal claims be re-phrased to fit only one model? Donald Davidson
has championed the view that only events stand in causal relations (thereby providing
another reason to believe in an **ontology** of events); hence (i) and (ii) should be
re-written along the lines of (iii).[1] I take no view on this issue, though all examples of
singular causation in this chapter will involve events.

DAVID HUME (1711–1776)

Born in Berwickshire, Scotland, Hume is generally regarded as the greatest ever English-speaking philosopher. He was also a noted historian and essayist. Following in the tradition of Locke and Berkeley, Hume was an **empiricist**, a naturalist and a sceptic. His major philosophical works – *A Treatise of Human Nature* (1739–40), *Enquiry Concerning Human Understanding* (1748), *Enquiry Concerning the Principles of Morals* (1751), as well as the posthumously published *Dialogues Concerning Natural Religion* (1779) – were influential, though criticized at the time as works of scepticism and atheism. Hume's eventual fame and fortune was largely due to the publication of his six-volume *History of England* (1754–62). His reputation for atheism prevented his election to chairs in Edinburgh (1745) and Glasgow (1752). He never held an academic post. An agreeable and clubbable man, Hume was friends with the leading intellectuals of his time. He could count Adam Smith, James Boswell, Denis Diderot and (briefly) Jean-Jacques Rousseau among his friends and acquaintances.

• HUME

Modern discussion of causation begins with David Hume. However, Hume was concerned not just with causation but also with the origin of the idea of cause in our minds. This latter question was pressing given Hume's commitment to the following empiricist principle:

(EP) Every idea is either simple or complex. Complex ideas are constructions out of simple ones. Simple ideas derive from impressions (of sensation or reflection).

In the *Treatise of Human Nature*, Hume identifies three elements in our idea of causation:

(i) *Contiguity*: causes and effects are adjacent in space and time.
If a brick hits a window and causes the window to smash, the two events – the brick hitting the window and the window smashing – are adjacent to each other in time and space. Of course, we also talk of my throwing the brick as causing the window to smash, and those events are not contiguous. But those events are linked by intermediate chains of cause and effect, each link of which connects contiguous elements.

(ii) *Priority*: a cause must precede its effect.
Condition (ii) rules out the possibility of backwards or even simultaneous causation. This is apt to seem a stipulation on Hume's part, though not an arbitrary one. Without it, Hume would be unable to specify, of a pair of contiguous events, which was the cause and which the effect.

Hume accepts (i) and (ii) as essential to causation, but concedes that we cannot define causation only in terms of them. This is surely correct. For example, suppose my dog barks when I throw a brick at a window. The soundwaves of the bark are prior to, and contiguous with, the window-smashing, yet they do not cause the window to smash. What more is required? Hume suggests:

(iii) *Necessity*: if A causes B there is a necessary connection between A and B.
This is a plausible condition. If I throw a brick and it hits the window, we don't think that it just so happens that the window smashes; we think the window must smash. The barking plainly does not necessitate the smash – as we could empirically test.

Cause and effect are necessarily connected. But what kind of necessity is this? Not logical necessity: there is no logical contradiction in the eventuality of a brick just bouncing off a window. This may never happen, but such an eventuality is conceivable. The necessity in question is not logical but natural necessity, and the idea of such necessity is essential to our idea of causation.

How did we acquire this idea of necessity? From what impression does it derive? Hume says that when he observes particular instances of cause and effect, all he perceives are the contiguity and succession of events – one thing followed by another. From the observation of a single conjunction, we cannot derive the idea of necessity. But from observation of multiple conjunctions we can acquire this idea. Upon exposure to many cases of As being followed by Bs, and observing no counterinstances, we come to expect future As to be followed by Bs, and thus we form the idea of necessary connection.

According to Hume, then, the idea of necessary connection is a copy of an impression in our minds, not a copy of any feature in the external world. Upon repeated exposure to conjoined types of events in the world, we naturally form certain feelings of expectation and anticipation, and from those feelings we derive the idea of necessary connection. Our natural belief that there is necessity in the world is a **projection** of the mind onto the world.

HUME'S PROJECTIVISM

According to Hume, ideas are copies of impressions, and the idea of causation involves the idea of necessity. From what impression does the idea of necessity derive? Not from exposure to just one instance of an event of one type being followed by an event of another type. It is only after repeated exposure to such conjunctions that the mind forms the idea of necessary connection. The impression of necessity must therefore be an internal impression (consisting in feelings of expectation and anticipation) brought about by the mind's exposure to constant conjunctions. We mistakenly project this necessity back onto the world, giving rise to the illusion that necessary connections hold between events in the external world. So runs the standard interpretation of Hume on causation, according to which Hume is a projectivist rather than a **realist** about causation. However, recently some philosophers (such as Galen Strawson) have questioned this interpretation.

Hume offered two definitions of 'cause'. These definitions are not equivalent, yet together they encapsulate Hume's understanding of the idea of cause. According to the first definition, a cause is 'an object, followed by another, and where all objects similar to the first are followed by objects similar to the second'.[2] According to the second definition, a cause is 'an object followed by another, ... whose appearance always conveys the thought to that other'.[3] Neither definition makes reference to necessity, presumably because there is no worldly necessity to make our causal claims true.

• THE REGULARITY THEORY

It was the first definition that gave rise to what has become known as the regularity theory of causation. We can state the theory as follows:

> (RT) A caused B **if and only if** (i) A preceded B and (ii) all A-type events are followed by B-type events.[4]

The regularity theory is intended to be a **reductive** account of causation. That is, claims (i) and (ii) are intended to be intelligible independently of the notion of causation. Hence, a problematic concept (causation) comes to be understood in terms of supposedly less problematic concepts (precedence and regularity). (RT) is intended as a necessary truth, covering all possible cases of causation.

There are two broad ways in which the regularity theory might be criticized. It may be false or it may fail to be reductive (or both). There are two ways in which it might be false. First, there might be a case where (i) and (ii) are true yet A did not cause B ((RT) fails right to left). Second, there might be a case where A caused B but either (i) or (ii) is false ((RT) fails left to right). I think the regularity theory can be criticized in both these ways.

(RT) fails right to left

There are a number of ways in which (i) and (ii) may be satisfied, yet A not cause B. For example, Thomas Reid (1710–1796) pointed out that '[i]t follows from [Hume's] definition of a cause, that night is the cause of day, and day the cause of night. For no two things have more constantly followed each other since the beginning of the world.'[5] This, of course, is the wrong result: day does not cause night, nor vice versa; rather day and night are joint effects of a common cause (the Earth's rotation on its axis).

(RT) fails left to right

Are there cases where A causes B yet either (i) or (ii) fail? (RT) implies that a cause always precedes its effect. Hence, if simultaneous or backwards causation is possible then (RT) is false. There are plausible examples of simultaneous causation in our world – e.g., the impact of a sphere landing on a cushion causing the cushion to change shape. It is arguable that backwards causation is also possible, even if it never occurs in our world (see below).

Putting the possibility of simultaneous or backwards causation to one side, condition (ii) raises another interesting issue. (RT) is a classic generalist theory: true singular causal claims are held always to be underwritten by exceptionless generalizations.[6] In contrast, singularist philosophers of causation – most notably, G.E.M. Anscombe – think that from the fact that A caused B it does not follow that there must be a true and exceptionless generalization to the effect that all A-type events are followed by B-type events. Anscombe rejects the Humean assumption that '[i]f an effect occurs in one case and a similar effect does not occur in an apparently similar case, there must be a relevant further difference.'[7] That is, it can be true that A causes B even though clause (ii) is false.

Here are four reasons to prefer singularism to generalism:

(a) Clauses of type (ii) will almost always be false. If you claim that A caused B and 'then construct a universal proposition "Always, given an A, a B follows", you usually won't get anything true. You have got to describe the absence of circumstances in which an A would not cause a B. But the task of excluding all such circumstances can't be carried out.'[8]

(b) Nothing in the concept of causation forces generalism upon us. There seems to be no conceptual infelicity in someone endorsing a singular causal claim, yet refusing to endorse any corresponding general claim. For example, one seems to make no conceptual mistake in conceding that Carol developed cancer whilst refusing to assert that anyone in biologically similar circumstances would also develop cancer.

Developments in 20th-century physics, at least on some interpretations, provide concrete examples to support this idea. If there are causal transactions at the quantum level, and if quantum interactions are **indeterministic**, then there actually are cause–effect pairs which do not fall under exceptionless generalizations of the 'All As are Bs' variety. For example, the emission of some particle may have been caused by the prior state of some radioactive material, yet it's not true that a similar particle is emitted whenever similar material is in a similar state.

(c) Generalism implies that whether A causes B depends on whether, at any time in the past or future, an A-type event fails to be followed by a B-type event. This is counter-intuitive. Intuitively, what makes it true that Oswald shot Kennedy are the local events involving Oswald and Kennedy at the relevant time and place. Other shootings are irrelevant. Singularism respects this intuition.

(d) Generalism has two untoward epistemic consequences.

 (i) According to generalism, A caused B only if all A-type events are followed by B-type events. Since we cannot survey all space and time, we can never be sure of the latter generalization. Consequently, and absurdly, we can never conclusively assert the truth of any singular causal claim.

(ii) Generalists must hold that causation is not perceivable in individual instances. (Hume, of course, held this.) This consequence is implausible. As a singularist, Anscombe holds that causation is directly observable in individual instances. Given that we perceive material bodies, i.e., entities imbued with causal powers, she writes, 'what theory of perception can justly disallow the perception of a lot of causality?'[9] On Anscombe's view, we often experience or observe causation, e.g., when we will our arms to move, or when we see the knife cut the butter.

Is (RT) reductive?

(RT) is intended to be a reductive account of causation. It purports to explain causation in terms of temporal precedence and regularity, neither of which are presumed to presuppose causation. However, there is a third notion present in (RT): that of a *type* of event ('all A-type events are followed by B-type events'). What is it for an event to be an event of a particular type? Hume's answer invokes the notion of similarity. A particular event counts as an A-type event if it is similar to A.

But no two events are similar in all respects; so 'similarity' must mean 'similarity in relevant respects'. An A-type event is any event similar to A in relevant respects. But which respects are relevant? The danger looms that the relevant respects can be specified only as the causally relevant respects. Events are classified as A-type events, in part, because they bring about B-type events. But 'bring about' is a causal notion. If the individuation of event-types presupposes the notion of causation, the reductive aspirations of (RT) will be dashed.

• THE COUNTERFACTUAL THEORY

After Hume proposed his first definition of cause, he added the sentence: 'Or in other words, *if the first object had not been, the second never had existed.*' Many have found this addition puzzling since the idea it puts forward (that of a counterfactual connection between cause and effect) seems quite different from the idea behind the regularity theory of causation. The notion of a **counterfactual conditional** is logically quite different from the notion of a regularity or constant conjunction. It points to a new theory of causation, the counterfactual theory, the best-known advocate of which is David Lewis.[10]

According to the counterfactual theory:

(CT) A caused B if and only if, had A not happened, B wouldn't have happened.

Like (RT), (CT) is intended to be a reductive theory, and will be if the notion of a counterfactual can be understood independently of the notion of causation. Unlike (RT), however, (CT) is a singularist theory: no general claim has to be true in order for A to cause B. (On Lewis's **modal** realism, the only bit of reality relevant to the claim that A caused B is the most similar possible world to the actual world in which A failed to occur. If B failed to occur in that world, the causal claim is true. See Chapter 4.) Like Hume, but for different reasons, Lewis cannot hold that causation is perceptible; unlike Hume, he allows for the possibility of backwards causation.

(CT) makes essential use of a counterfactual conditional. We use counterfactuals regularly and unthinkingly. We all understand the counterfactual conditional 'if you had not been wearing a seatbelt, you would have been killed'. You were wearing a seatbelt (hence the **antecedent** of the conditional is counter to the facts), and you weren't killed; but if you hadn't been wearing a seatbelt, you would have been killed. We need not worry here about the correct analysis of counterfactuals. All we need draw on is our common sense understanding of the world and our grasp of the English language.

(CT) certainly fits most cases of causation. My turning the ignition key causes my motor to start; and had I not turned it, the motor would not have started. Fine. But to be true, (CT) must fit all cases of causation. Unfortunately, it doesn't. Two types of case yield counterexamples to (CT): pre-emption and over-determination. In both types of case (CT) fails left to right. That is, they are both types of case in which A causes B, but in which it is not true that, had A not happened, B would not have happened.

Pre-emption cases

Pre-emption cases are cases where A causes B (there is only one line of causation), but had A not occurred, C would have occurred instead and brought about B. Suppose that, as a result of hypnosis, the neurotic New Yorker Nancy will jump out of her (14th floor) apartment window if her phone rings at 8 a.m. Imagine that, knowing this, Bill rings her at 8 a.m., causing her to jump out of the window. Fred, who also dislikes Nancy, is waiting in the wings in case Bill should fail to call (but does not have to intervene).

Bill's calling caused Nancy to jump out of the window. But had Bill not called, the very same sequence of events would have ensued (since Fred would have called instead). So Bill's call caused Nancy's jump, but it's not true that had Bill not called, Nancy wouldn't have jumped. (A nice feature of this example, unlike other examples of pre-emption, is that the relevant actual sequence of events – from Bill dialling to Nancy jumping – is identical to the counterfactual sequence from Fred dialling to Nancy jumping. Had Fred called, Nancy's jump would have been brought about in the very same way.)

Over-determination cases

Over-determination cases are cases where A and B cause C, and where either would have done so in the absence of the other. (Suppose that Nancy has two phones, and that either ringing by itself would cause her to jump. Simultanously Bill calls one phone while Fred calls the other, causing her to jump.) In a case of over-determination, the effect C is not counterfactually dependent upon A or upon B. If A hadn't happened, C would still have happened; and if B hadn't happened, C would still have happened. Hence, according to (CT), A didn't cause C and B didn't cause C. But this is counterintuitive: surely A caused C and B caused C.

In cases of under-determination – where X and Y together cause Z, but neither would have done so by itself – the verdict of (CT) is in accord with common sense (i.e., not true that X caused Z or Y caused Z). In cases of over-determination, in contrast, there are two sufficient lines of causation, so each cause brought about the effect. But (CT) cannot acknowledge this datum.

ELIZABETH ANSCOMBE (1919–2001)

Gertrude Elizabeth Margaret Anscombe studied at St Hugh's College, Oxford, and later attended lectures at Cambridge given by the Austrian philosopher Ludwig Wittgenstein. She became a close friend of Wittgenstein, translated his *Philosophical Investigations* (1953) and was nominated as one of his literary executors. She was subsequently appointed to Wittgenstein's old chair at Cambridge, which she occupied from 1970 until her retirement in 1986. Apart from her translations of Wittgenstein, Anscombe is best known for *Intention* (1957), *Three Philosophers* (1963) (written jointly with her husband, the philosopher and logician P.T. Geach), and three volumes of collected papers, ranging over topics in the history of philosophy, metaphysics, philosophy of mind, ethics and religion. A controversial figure, she opposed the entry of Britain into the Second World War (on the grounds that civilians would deliberately be killed), and was fiercely opposed to contraception and abortion.

• ANSCOMBE'S PROPOSAL

(RT) and (CT) are flawed theories. They fix on contingencies which happen to be true in most cases of causation, but are not of the essence of causation. Causes and effects do typically exhibit a regular pattern, and effects are typically counterfactually dependent on their causes. But neither theory captures our notion of causation.

Since neither theory is satisfactory, we should consider an alternative theory, or sketch of a theory, proposed by Elizabeth Anscombe. As noted earlier, Anscombe is a singularist about causation, and holds that causation is perceptible in individual instances. She offers the following remarks about causation: 'causality consists in the derivativeness of an effect from its causes. This is the core, the common feature, of causality in its various kinds. Effects derive from, arise out of, come of, their causes.'[11] Paradigm examples of derivation would be an animal deriving from (being generated by) its parents, or an oak-tree deriving from (growing from) an acorn. Neither the notion of a regularity nor of a counterfactual dependency can do justice to the idea of derivation.

Anscombe's proposal can be stated simply:

(AT) A causes B if and only if B derives from A.

The notion of derivation is meant to capture the idea that an effect is generated by, or produced by, its cause. Anscombe distinguishes necessitating from non-necessitating causes. A necessitating cause is one where 'if C occurs it is certain to cause E unless something prevents it. ... If "certainty" should seem too epistemological a notion: a necessitating cause C of a given kind of effect E is such that it is not possible (on the occasion) that C should occur and should not cause an E, given that there is nothing that prevents an E from occuring.'[12] Necessitating causes are, for example, those underwritten by **laws of nature**. Thus, it is necessitated that a brick will fall to earth when dropped – unless something prevents it.

A non-necessitating cause is 'one that can fail of its effect without the intervention of anything to frustrate it'.[13] A nice example of a non-necessitating cause is the explosion of a bomb caused by the undetermined emission of a particle from some radio-active material. The explosion is caused, and derives from its cause, but there was no necessity for the bomb to explode at the time it did. It could have failed to explode at that time without anything preventing it.

Anscombe offers no reduction of the notion of derivation. The relation of derivation cannot be identified with the relation of natural necessity (since not all causes necessitate). Nor is every case of derivation underwritten by an exceptionless generalization (since Anscombe is a singularist, and believes in non-necessitating causes).

CAUSATION: REDUCIBLE OR BASIC?

If a property or relation is thought to be problematic, philosophers often attempt to domesticate it by reducing it to more basic, less problematic, components. Thus, for example, knowledge was long held to be reducible to justified true belief. Many have thought that causation is similarly reducible – either to regularities in nature or to counterfactual dependencies. On the regularity theory, A caused B if and only if A precedes B and A-type events are always followed by B-type events. On the counterfactual theory, A caused B if and only if, had A not happened, B wouldn't have happened either. Unfortunately, both theories are open to counterexamples, so neither theory is tenable. But there is another possibility. Perhaps the causal relation is primitive, and so not reducible to more basic elements. On one view, causation is derivation, where the derivation of an effect from its cause is not itself reducible to regularities, counterfactual dependencies, or to anything else.

• A NOTE ON BACKWARDS CAUSATION

The question of whether backwards causation is possible is important in itself, and also relevant to our discussions of time travel and fatalism (see Chapters 8 and 10, respectively). One backwards causation scenario imagines the history of the universe to be a giant **causal loop** so that for any two events, A and B, if A causes B, B is part of a chain of events which loops round to cause A. However, our concern is with a less exotic possibility: a universe in which causation is typically from earlier to later, but occasionally in the reverse direction.

Michael Dummett provides a nice example: 'A man is observed regularly to wake up three minutes before his alarm-clock goes off. ... Whenever the alarm has been set and wound, but fails to go off because of some mechanical accident, which is later discovered, he always sleeps very late.'[14] Provided that there is no alternative explanation of his waking, and provided that his waking is no part of the explanation of the alarm going off, then it need not be irrational to deem the alarm going off the cause of his waking three minutes earlier (as opposed to regarding the regularity as a mere coincidence).

As we have seen, Hume's definition of cause rules out backwards causation; but that seems an unwarranted stipulation on Hume's part. Kant thought it a synthetic *a priori* truth that a cause precedes its effect. But Kant also thought it a synthetic *a priori* truth that space is three-dimensional and that every event has a cause – claims no longer regarded as *a priori* or even true.

Anscombe's theory is compatible with backwards causation. Lewis, as a defender of the possibility of time travel, also takes his theory to be compatible with backwards causation (though there are some technical difficulties due to the way Lewis understands counterfactuals). Given our criticisms in previous sections, we have found no theory of causation which is both plausible and rules out backwards causation.

Black's challenge

However, some have thought that, independently of any theory of causation, backwards causation is open to objection. In 1956 Max Black presented the so-called bilking argument against the possibility of backwards causation.[15] Suppose, for *reductio*, that L-events cause earlier E-events. Suppose we observe an E-event and then try to prevent its cause from occurring (i.e., we attempt to bilk). If successful, this would undermine the claim of that E-event to be caused by an L-event. Since such intervention is always possible, L-events cannot cause E-events, and thus backwards causation is impossible.

It is hard to feel the force of this reasoning. First, it does nothing to show the impossibility of backwards causation in agent-free worlds. Second, the reasoning is confused. Suppose a particular event E* occurs, purportedly caused by a later event L*. Having seen E* occur, I attempt to prevent the occurrence of L*. There are two possibilities:

(i)   I succeed in ensuring that L* does not occur. In that case L* was not the cause of
      E*. Does this show that E* was not backwardly caused? No; some other later
      event might have caused it.

(ii) I try to prevent L* but fail. Obviously this does not show that E* was not caused
      by L*. (I take it we have ruled out E* being a cause of L*.) If L* is the cause of E*,
      then clearly L* will occur if E* has occurred, and so will not be prevented. Might
      I have prevented L*? In other circumstances perhaps, but not consistently with
      the assumptions that E* occurred and was caused by L*.

Equally, in a normal case where the earlier A causes the later B, I cannot, upon
observing A, prevent B. This is not some fatalistic constraint on my powers; it is
simply the consequence of adhering to a consistent description.

• CONCLUDING REMARKS

The two standard reductive theories of causation, the regularity theory and the
counterfactual theory, are open to a range of objections. An alternative is
Anscombe's derivation view of causation. Although the notion of derivation
needs further development, Anscombe's proposal does seem to capture a key
aspect of causation. Anscombe's theory is consistent with cases of backwards
causation. The possibility of backwards causation is not undermined by the
so-called bilking argument.

• STUDY QUESTIONS

- What are the *relata* of the causal relation?
- How plausible is Hume's empiricist principle (EP)?
- What is the most telling objection to the regularity theory?
- Why are cases of pre-emption and over-determination problems for the counter-
  factual theory?
- Is there a plausible version of the bilking argument against backwards causation?

• ANNOTATED FURTHER READING

G.E.M. Anscombe, 'Causality and Determination', in *Metaphysics and the Philosophy
of Mind* (Oxford: Basil Blackwell, 1981), pp. 133–48. A trenchant anti-Humean
tract. Anscombe argues that singular causal claims do not presuppose exceptionless generalizations, and that causation can be directly perceived. She also
makes a positive proposal about causation. A difficult paper.

M. Dummett, 'Can an Effect Precede its Cause?' (1954), reprinted in *Truth and
Other Enigmas* (Cambridge, Mass.: Harvard University Press, 1978), pp. 319–33.
A sympathetic introduction to the topic of backwards causation.

P. Horwich, 'Lewis's Programme', in *Asymmetries in the Philosophy of Time* (Cambridge, Mass.: MIT Press, 1987), pp. 129–47. A useful, if demanding, critique of Lewis's counterfactual theory of causation.

D. Lewis, 'Causation', reprinted in *Philosophical Papers*, Vol. II (Oxford: Oxford University Press, 1986), pp. 159–214. The classic source of counterfactual approaches to causation. A difficult read.

E. Sosa and M. Tooley (eds), *Causation* (Oxford: Oxford University Press, 1993). A useful collection with a readable introduction.

G. Strawson, *The Secret Connexion* (Oxford and New York: Clarendon Press, 1989). Strawson makes a detailed case for interpreting Hume as a realist about causation.

R. Teichmann, *The Philosophy of Elizabeth Anscombe* (Oxford: Oxford University Press, 2008). A useful introduction to Anscombe's philosophy, with some helpful pages on Anscombe's thoughts about causation.

• INTERNET RESOURCES

Jan Faye, 'Backward Causation', *The Stanford Encyclopedia of Philosophy* (Spring 2010 Edition), ed. Edward N. Zalta, URL = <http://plato.stanford.edu/archives/spr2010/entries/causation-backwards/>.

D. Garrett (2005), 'Hume, David', *Routledge Encyclopedia of Philosophy*, ed. E. Craig. Retrieved 31 May 2006 from <http://www.rep.routledge.com/article/DB040>.

P. Menzies (2001), 'Counterfactual Theories of Causation', *The Stanford Encyclopedia of Philosophy* (Spring 2001 edition), ed. Edward N. Zalta. Retrieved 31 May 2006 from <http://plato.stanford.edu/archives/spr2001/entries/causation-counterfactual>.

William Edward Morris, 'David Hume', *The Stanford Encyclopedia of Philosophy* (Summer 2009 Edition), ed. Edward N. Zalta, URL = <http://plato.stanford.edu/archives/sum2009/entries/hume/>.

J. Schaffer (2003), 'The Metaphysics of Causation', *The Stanford Encyclopedia of Philosophy* (Spring 2003 edition), ed. Edward N. Zalta. Retrieved 31 May 2006 from <http://plato. stanford.edu/archives/spr2003/entries/causation-metaphysics>.

• NOTES

1. See, e.g., 'The Individuation of Events' and 'Causal Relations' reprinted in *Essays on Actions and Events* (Oxford: Clarendon Press, 2001), 2nd edn.
2. *Enquiry Concerning Human Understanding*, in *Enquiries concerning Human Understanding and concerning the Principles of Morals*, ed. L.A. Selby-Bigge, 3rd edn revised by P.H. Nidditch (Oxford: Clarendon Press, 1975), p. 76.
3. *Ibid.*, p. 77.
4. Note there is no requirement here that cause and effect be contiguous in space. This is relevant to an objection to Dualism (see Chapter 2).
5. T. Reid, *Essays on the Active Powers of the Human Mind*, ed. Baruch A. Brody (Cambridge, Mass.: MIT Press, 1969), p. 334

6. Donald Davidson is a modern defender of generalism about causation; it is a premise in his argument for anomalous monism. See 'Mental Events' reprinted in his *Essays on Actions and Events* (*op. cit.*).

7. G.E.M. Anscombe, 'Causality and Determination', in her *Metaphysics and the Philosophy of Mind* (Oxford: Basil Blackwell, 1981), p. 133.

8. *Ibid.*, p. 138.

9. *Ibid.*, p. 137.

10. D. Lewis, 'Causation', reprinted in his *Philosophical Papers*, Vol. II (Oxford: Oxford University Press, 1986).

11. Anscombe, *op. cit.*, p. 136.

12. *Ibid.*, p. 144.

13. *Ibid.*, p. 144.

14. M. Dummett, 'Can an Effect Precede its Cause?' (1954) reprinted in *Truth and Other Enigmas* (Cambridge, Mass.: Harvard University Press, 1978), p. 323.

15. M. Black, 'Why Cannot an Effect Precede its Cause?', *Analysis*, 16 (1956), 49–58.

8

˙time: the fundamental issue

• INTRODUCTION

In this chapter, we are concerned with a fundamental question about our world: what is the nature of time? Does time – in contrast to space – have an intrinsic direction and flow? Is there a moving *now*? Are past, present and future equally real? We will attempt to answer these questions by assessing the two major and opposing theories of time.

A THEORY/B THEORY

There are two theories of the nature of time: the A theory and the B theory. According to the A theory, time is dynamic. Time flows, and the moving *now* is the cutting edge of being. A theorists are either Presentists or Growing Universe theorists. On either view the future is unreal, and **contingent** statements about the future have no truth value. According to the B theory, time does not flow, and past, present and future are equally real. Contingent statements about the future are true or false, even if we don't always know which. On the B theory, time has no intrinsic direction or flow. There is no moving *now*, and utterances of 'now' merely refer to their times of utterance, just as utterances of 'here' refer to their places of utterance.

• A THEORY VS B THEORY

The B theory

According to the B theory, past, present and future are equally real; time, like space, does not flow; there is no moving *now* ('now' is a pure **indexical**, any utterance of which refers to its time of utterance). A description of reality in B series terms – that is, descriptions incorporating dates (such as 16 May 1961) and the relations 'earlier than' and 'later than' – suffices for a complete description of reality. We can still use A series terms – such as 'past', 'present' and 'future' – but they are not necessary to describe reality. For example, my 2012 utterance 'Stalin's death is past' is true just if Stalin's death is earlier than 2012; my 2012 utterance 'Obama's death is future' is true just if Obama's death is later than 2012; and my utterance on 1 February 2012 'it's raining now' is true just if it's raining on 1 February 2012. Sentences containing A series terms are true in virtue of the underlying B series facts.

The A theory

According to the A theory, in contrast, reality is constantly changing simply by virtue of the passage of time. Time literally flows – the *now* is a real and moving entity, separating being from non-being. A description of reality in B series terms is not complete, since it cannot answer the question 'what is happening now?'

The A theorist cannot hold that past, present and future are equally real, since the A theory would then collapse into the B theory. If past, present and future were real, no work would be done by the moving *now*. The *now* would not then be the moving divider between being and non-being. Since all theories of time hold the present to be real, and since it would be bizarre to hold the present and future real yet the past unreal, the only two serious versions of the A theory are Presentism and the Growing Universe View.

According to Presentism, only the present is real; past and future events do not exist. The present moment thus has an absolutely privileged status. Presentism is a radical doctrine and should not be confused with the truism that past and future events are not happening now.

According to the Growing Universe View, held by the Cambridge metaphysician C.D. Broad (1887–1971) amongst others, the present and past are real, but the future is unreal. The temporal extent of the universe is constantly expanding.

Time and modality

There are parallels between time and modality (see Chapter 4). Modal **realism** holds that all possible worlds are real and hence that the actual world has no privileged status; the B theory holds that all times are real and hence that the present moment has no privileged status. (It is no coincidence that David Lewis was both a modal realist and a B theorist.) Actualism holds that the actual world is the only **concrete** world that exists; Presentism holds that only the present is real. However, these parallels should not be taken to constitute arguments for particular theories.

In order to decide which theory of time is correct, we will look at some of the objections to each theory. J.M.E. McTaggart (1866–1925) had objections to both theories, and his discussion has largely set the terms of subsequent debate about time. We begin with his objection to the B theory.

J.M.E. McTAGGART (1866–1925)

John McTaggart was born in Wiltshire, England. He studied and taught at Trinity College, Cambridge, for most of his life (where his pupils included Bertrand Russell). In his most famous paper 'The Unreality of Time' (*Mind*, 1908) he distinguished two ways of ordering events in time, the A series and the B series. He argued that the A series is fundamental to time, but leads to contradiction. He concluded that time is unreal, and that what we perceive as events in a time-series really form a non-temporal C series. This conclusion – that what is real is timeless and unchanging – has impressive historical credentials, ranging from Plato to Hegel. McTaggart held that the spatio-temporal world was an illusion, and that reality consisted of immaterial souls in ecstatic communion with each other. McTaggart lived in metaphysically interesting times. Along with F.C. Bradley (1846–1924), McTaggart was a leading member of the school of Hegel-influenced British Idealism which flourished at the end of the 19th and early 20th centuries.

• McTAGGART'S OBJECTION TO THE B THEORY

McTaggart introduces his discussion by observing that:

> Positions in time, as time appears to us *prima facie*, are distinguished in two ways. Each position is Earlier than some and Later than some of the other positions. ... In the second place, each position is either Past, Present or Future. The distinctions of the former class are permanent, while those of the latter are not. If M is ever earlier than N, it is always earlier. But an event, which is now present, was future, and will be past.[1]

It was the permanency of B series locations and relations, McTaggart thought, which yielded a decisive objection to the B theory. Events never change their B series location (e.g., it always was and always will be true that Hitler's death occurred in 1945). Nor do they change their B series relations to other events (e.g., it always was and always will be true that Hitler's death is later than Caesar's death). This, for McTaggart, shows that the B series cannot allow for change. No theory of time can be tenable if it fails to allow for change.

The only respect in which an event – McTaggart's example is the death of Queen Anne – can change is in the following respect: '[i]t began by being a future event. It became every moment an event in the nearer future. At last it was present. Then it became past, and will always remain so, though every moment it becomes further and further past.'[2] Hence, McTaggart concluded, change is possible only on the A series.

Russell's reply

Bertrand Russell was a B theorist. He held, against McTaggart, that the B theory is compatible with change:

> Change is the difference, in respect of truth or falsehood, between a proposition concerning an entity and the time T, and a proposition concerning the same entity and the time T*, provided that these propositions differ only by the fact that T occurs in the one where T* occurs in the other.[3]

There is change if, e.g., the proposition 'at time T my poker is hot' is true, and the proposition 'at time T* my poker is hot' is false. More simply, there is change if my poker is hot at one time and cold at some other time. Change, so understood, requires only the B series.

According to McTaggart, however, Russell's account is not an account of change. For the proposition 'at time T my poker is hot', if true, is always true, and the proposition 'at time T* my poker is hot', if false, is always false. This makes no change in the qualities of the poker. It is true at all times that the poker is hot at T and that it is cold at T*. This permanency in truth value, for McTaggart, implies that there is no change to the poker.

How should we adjudicate this dispute? We are being offered two quite different accounts of change: 'McTaggart change' and 'Russell change'. McTaggart change occurs whenever an event alters its A series position. Russell change occurs whenever an object has incompatible properties at different times. We need to ask the question: is Russell change recognizable as a notion of change?

On the face of it, 'yes'. An object's altering its properties – e.g., my garden gate being green on Monday and then painted red on Tuesday – ordinarily counts as a change. In order for change to occur, we don't require that the event of the painting change. We simply require the object to have changed its properties. In which case Russell's reply stands, and McTaggart's argument against the B theory crumbles.

CHANGE

What is change? According to Bertrand Russell, change is an object's having incompatible properties at different times. If my garden gate is green on Monday and then painted red on Tuesday, it has changed. According to J.M.E. McTaggart, change occurs not to objects but to events. No event can change its B series location: that is fixed and permanent. An event changes only in respect of its A series position: it was future, then briefly present, then past for evermore. Hence, McTaggart concluded, change is possible only on the A theory. But many have held that 'Russell change' is our ordinary notion of change. No event need change in order for an object to change. Hence, the B theory can accommodate change.

• McTAGGART'S PARADOX

It is often said that the A theory is the intuitive or common sense view of time. Not only does time flow but we directly experience the flow of time. It is doubtful whether the phenomenological evidence supports this conclusion. Even if it did, experiences can be deceptive. Despite its naturalness, there are a number of formidable objections to the A theory.

In a famous discussion, McTaggart wrote:

> Past, present and future are incompatible determinations. ... But every event has them all. If M is past, it has been present and future. If it is future, it will be present and past. If it is present, it has been future and will be past.[4]

We can represent McTaggart's reasoning as follows:

(1)   Every event is past, present and future.

(2)   No event can be past, present and future. So:

(3)   The A series is contradictory.

The thought behind (1) is that no event escapes the passage of time: any event is future, then fleetingly present, then past for evermore. Every event occupies every A series position. (There will be exceptions, if there is a first or last event. But this does not affect the argument since the first event would still be present and past, and the last event future and present, and these determinations are incompatible.)

The thought behind (2) is that past, present and future are incompatible determinations: if an event is past it is not present or future, if it is present it is not past or future, and so on. Nothing can possess incompatible characteristics. From (1) and (2), (3) follows.

Responses to McTaggart's Paradox

(i) An obvious reply?

Now it might seem that there is an obvious reply to this argument. Indeed McTaggart states the reply himself:

> It is never true, the answer will run, that M is present, past and future. It is present, *will be* past, and *has been* future. Or it is past, and has been future and present, or again *is* future and *will be* present and past. The characteristics are only incompatible when they are simultaneous, and there is no contradiction to this in the fact that each term has all of them successively.[5]

In other words: we avoid the charge of contradiction in the first-level A series positions (M is past, present and future) by invoking three consistent positions in a second-level A series (e.g., M is present, was future, and will be past).

McTaggart's counter

However, McTaggart counters that there are nine positions in the second-level A series (is past, is present, is future, was past, was present, was future, will be past, will be present, will be future) and every event occupies all of these A series positions. Some combinations of these nine positions are incompatible (e.g., is present and is past). We can overcome these contradictions by distinguishing more complex tenses, and moving up to third-level A series positions. But every event occupies every A series position and some of these 27 positions are incompatible. To avoid contradiction we must move up to a fourth level, and so on without end. We can escape contradiction by moving up a level, but at every level a contradiction remains.

Here is a simpler way of presenting McTaggart's counter: the obvious reply makes use of the B series terms 'simultaneously' and 'successively'. To render the passage of time consistent, the A theorist must use only A series terms. Yet the attempt to do so leads to a **vicious regress**.

(ii) Presentism escapes the paradox

Presentism seems to escape entirely McTaggart's Paradox. If only present events are real, then (1) is simply false. McTaggart assumed that an A theorist should hold past, present and future to be equally real. (For example, he talks of Queen Anne's death being future, then present, then past, and he criticized C.D. Broad for denying the reality of the future.) McTaggart would not have regarded Presentism as a tenable version of the A theory.

Unlike McTaggart, I think that the A theorist should not hold past, present and future to be equally real. I take Presentism and the Growing Universe View to be the only versions of the A theory worth considering. Since Presentism escapes the paradox, that leaves the Growing Universe View. Despite holding past and present events to be real, a defender of that view has no reason to be worried by McTaggart's Paradox.

M.A.E. DUMMETT (1925 TO PRESENT)

Sir Michael Dummett was born in London in 1925. After serving in the Second World War, he studied at Christ Church, Oxford, before being elected a Prize Fellow of All Souls in 1950. In 1979 he became Wykeham Professor of Logic and a Fellow of New College, a position he held until retirement in 1992. A committed Catholic and social activist, Dummett was especially involved in anti-racism campaigns in Britain during the 1960s. The two major influences on Dummett's philosophy are Frege and Wittgenstein. He has written three substantial tomes on Frege's philosophy of language and philosophy of mathematics. Dummett has also developed the view that traditional debates in metaphysics can be advanced, and perhaps even resolved, by focusing on debates in the theory of meaning. Here the Wittgensteinian doctrine of the public nature of meaning (and the corresponding impossibility of a private language) has had a great effect on Dummett's thinking. Dummett is still an active philosopher and has recently published two more books: *Truth and the Past* (2005) and *Thought and Reality* (2006).

(iii) The Growing Universe View defended against the paradox

In his illuminating discussion of the paradox, Michael Dummett holds that McTaggart makes an implicit assumption.[6] He assumes that, irrespective of one's position in time, it must be possible to give a consistent description of reality which includes all A series truths.

However, when we try to specify all the A series truths, as opposed to specifying those which are true from one particular perspective, we end up in contradiction. Given the assumption that it must be possible to specify all A series truths, whatever one's position in time, McTaggart concluded that the A series is contradictory.

Should a Growing Universe theorist accept that it is possible to specify all A series truths, independently of one's temporal perspective? No. It is essential to the Growing Universe View that the fundamental temporal facts (i.e., the **tensed facts** which record an event's position in the A series) change as time passes. Reality is constantly being repartitioned: facts that are present become past; facts that are past become more past. I can state the facts as they are from the present perspective including, e.g., the fact that I am alive. One hundred years hence a different set of facts will obtain, including the fact that I am dead.

There is only a contradiction if we assume that there is some true perspective-neutral description which includes both facts. The Growing Universe theorist should deny that there can be such a description. Any description of temporal reality, from a perspective within time, is necessarily incomplete. Thus premise (1) is false: from any perspective in time, each event has only one A series position.

In denying (1), the Growing Universe theorist embraces the relativity of tensed truths. Tensed truths are perspectival. It is not true *simpliciter*, e.g., that my birth is past. It is true relative to the current perspective, but false relative to the perspective of one thousand years ago. Dummett admits it is not easy to give up the belief that there must be a complete or perspective-free description of reality. Nonetheless he is willing to take the moral of McTaggart's reasoning to be that we should 'abandon our prejudice that there must be a complete description of reality.'[7]

(iv) Horwich's defence of McTaggart's Paradox

Paul Horwich, in contrast, thinks that the completeness assumption should not be given up, and so concludes that McTaggart's paradox does refute the Growing Universe View.[8] According to Horwich, the A theorist's idea that there is 'a variation, from one time to another, as to which facts obtain' trades on 'an idiosyncratic and unmotivated conception of *fact*'.[9]

Horwich offers an example to support his claim. He says that:

we do not regard

X is to the left of Y

and

X is not to the left of Y

as explicit descriptions of facts. Rather we suppose that whenever such claims are true, they are partial accounts of facts whose explicit descriptions take the form

X is to the left of Y relative to Z

and

X is not to the left of Y relative to W ... .

The general point is that we reserve the term 'fact' for those aspects of reality whose explicit descriptions are sentences that are true *simpliciter* – and not merely true relative to some contexts or points of view, and false relative to others.[10]

Any A theorist should concede that there can be a complete or non-perspectival description of spatial facts. People with different positions in space can agree on all the spatial facts. This, after all, is why maps are useful: we don't need a different map for each location. But temporal facts do not admit of an observer-independent description. Hence, Horwich's example, far from telling against the A theory, highlights a fundamental difference between space and time. Or so says the A theorist.

● FOUR OBJECTIONS TO THE A THEORY

Two objections to any version of the A theory

(i) If time flows, how fast does it flow? One answer is that it flows at the plodding rate of one second per second. It will be objected that this is not a rate in the normal sense. A rate require two dimensions or parameters – e.g., 70 *miles* per *hour*. Some A theorists invoke a second-order time series relative to which the first-order series flows. So time flows at, e.g., a rate of 3 seconds of first-order time per 4 seconds of second-order time.

There are at least two problems with this. (a) It is hard to see how this rate could be specified in any non-arbitrary way. (b) The second-order time series also flows, and so we will need to invoke a third-order time series relative to which the second-order series flows, and so on *ad infinitum*. But surely there are not infinite orders of time.

(ii) A theorists assume that there is a single objective *now*, covering the entire universe. Yet considerations from special-relativity theory appear to show that there is no absolute and unique *now*. What is happening now is relative to one's frame of reference, and what is present in one frame of reference may be past or future in another. It's true that B theorists assume that there is only one B series, and that belief will have to be revised too. But a multiplicity of B series does not seem as problematic as a multiplicity of frame-relative *nows*. (McTaggart discusses the suggestion that there might be several independent A series, but thinks this would not be fatal to the A theory.[11])

An objection to Presentism

Presentism is the purest expression of the A theory – it assigns the present an utterly unique status. However, Presentism seems incompatible with the obvious fact that present events are caused by past ones. If X caused Y, X and Y must both exist; so it can't be true that only present events are real. Since present events are caused by past ones, it can't be true that only present events are real. Moreover, if there are no past facts, how can any past-tensed statement be true? How can memory be veracious?

An objection to the Growing Universe View

According to the Growing Universe View, the present is not ontologically privileged since past events are as real as present ones. However, the following problem confronts a view which combines a commitment to the moving *now* with a belief in the reality of the past. Consider the people and events of 1900. According to the Growing Universe View, they are as real as the people and events existing now. There is no ontological difference between us and them. The 1900 people believe that the things happening around them are happening now. But they are wrong, since 1900 is in the past. But if the 1900 people are wrong, maybe we are wrong too when we believe that we are living in the present. If past existence is as real as present existence then, for all we know, it could be that it is now 4000 AD and we are all living in the past. But this is absurd. Any theory of time which allows for the possibility that we are (literally) living in the past cannot be right. Yet the Growing Universe View is exactly such a theory.[12]

Victory to the B theory?

The B theory avoids all the above objections since it holds that past, present and future are equally real, and denies that there is a moving *now*. For example, on the B theory it is not possible that we are living in the past. Any utterance containing 'now' refers to its B series time of utterance. An utterance at time t of 'x is happening now' is true just if x occurs at t. If I say 'it's raining now' what I say is guaranteed to be true provided that it is indeed raining at the time of my utterance. It is impossible, on the B theory, for that utterance to be false because we are living in the past.

● CONCLUDING REMARKS

In this chapter, we have outlined the two leading theories of time: the A theory and the B theory. We looked at McTaggart's arguments against each theory and found both arguments wanting. Nonetheless, serious difficulties confront both versions of the A theory, leaving the B theory by far the more plausible view. However, as we shall see in the next chapter, it is not all plain sailing for the B theory.

● STUDY QUESTIONS

- How is the A theory to be distinguished from the B theory?
- Why did McTaggart think that change was possible only on the A theory?
- What is McTaggart's Paradox?
- Is time like space?
- What is the strongest objection to the A theory?

● ANNOTATED FURTHER READING

M. Dummett, 'A Defence of McTaggart's Proof of the Unreality of Time', in his *Truth and Other Enigmas* (Cambridge, Mass.: Harvard University Press, 1980), pp. 351–7. This is not a defence of McTaggart's Paradox, but a plea for the paradox to be taken seriously. Dummett thinks that McTaggart's Paradox, though it does not show time to be unreal, obliges us to give up an intuitive principle about the description of reality.

P. Horwich, *Asymmetries in Time* (Cambridge, Mass.: MIT Press, 1987), Chapter 2. A clear and engaging discussion of all the issues discussed here. Horwich takes McTaggart's Paradox to refute the A theory, but he disagrees with McTaggart over whether change is possible on the B theory.

R. Le Poidevin and M. MacBeath (eds), *The Philosophy of Time* (Oxford: Oxford University Press, 1993). A useful introduction by the editors, and reprints of classic discussions of time-related issues by (amongst others) McTaggart, Prior, Mellor, Shoemaker, Dummett, Lewis and Quinton.

J.M.E. McTaggart, 'The Unreality of Time', *Mind*, Vol. 17, No. 4, (1908), pp. 431–74. McTaggart's discussion oriented the 20th and 21st-century philosophical debate on time.

D.H. Mellor, *Real Time* (Cambridge: Cambridge University Press, 1998), 2nd edn, Chapter 6. Like Horwich, Mellor takes McTaggart's Paradox to undermine the A theory and holds that change is possible on the B theory. A vigorous defence of the B theory.

D.C. Williams, 'The Myth of Passage', *Journal of Philosophy*, Vol. 48 (1951), pp. 457–72. A spirited defence of the B theory of time and the 'block' universe.

• INTERNET RESOURCES

H. Dyke (2005), 'Time, Metaphysics of', *Routledge Encyclopedia of Philosophy*, ed. E. Craig. Retrieved 31 May 2006 from <http://www.rep.routledge.com/article/N123>.

N. Markosian (2002), 'Time', *The Stanford Encyclopedia of Philosophy* (Winter 2002 edition), ed. Edward N. Zalta. Retrieved 31 May 2006 from <http://plato.stanford.edu/ archives/win2002/entries/time>.

R. Le Poidevin (2005), 'Presentism', *Routledge Encyclopedia of Philosophy*, ed. E. Craig. Retrieved 31 May 2006 from <http://www.rep.routledge.com/article/N120>.

L. Sklar (1998), 'Time', *Routledge Encyclopedia of Philosophy*, ed. E. Craig. Retrieved 31 May 2006 from <http://www.rep.routledge.com/article/Q107>.

• NOTES

1. J.M.E. McTaggart, 'The Unreality of Time', *Mind*, Vol. 17, No. 4 (1908), p. 458.
2. *Ibid.*, p. 460.
3. B. Russell, *Principles of Mathematics* (Cambridge: Cambridge University Press; 2nd edn, Allen & Unwin, 1937), section 442.
4. McTaggart, *op. cit.*, p. 468.
5. *Ibid.*, p. 468.
6. M. Dummett, 'A Defence of McTaggart's Proof of the Unreality of Time', in his *Truth and Other Enigmas* (Cambridge, Mass.: Harvard University Press, 1978), pp. 351–8.
7. *Ibid.*, p. 357.
8. P. Horwich, *Asymmetries in Time: Problems in the Philosophy of Science* (Cambridge, Mass.: MIT Press, 1987), Chapter 2.
9. *Ibid.*, p. 22.
10. *Ibid.*, pp. 22–3.
11. McTaggart, *op. cit.*, p. 466.
12. For more on this objection, see D. Braddon-Mitchell 'How do we know it is now now?', *Analysis*, Vol. 64, No. 3 (2004), pp.199–203.

9

time: three puzzles

• INTRODUCTION

In this chapter I want to look at three interesting puzzles concerning time, two of which have implications for the debate about the nature of time. We will examine: (i) the character and significance of our temporally biased attitudes and utterances; (ii) Shoemaker on the possibility of time without change; and (iii) Lewis on the possibility of time travel. The existence of temporally biased attitudes, and the possibility of time without change, create difficulties for the B theory of time.

• TEMPORALLY BIASED ATTITUDES

We appear to have temporally biased attitudes towards our own experiences. We care more about our future experiences that we do about our past ones. We prefer painful experiences to be in the past, and pleasant experiences to be in the future. We often have no choice about the order in which we have experiences, so it can be hard to see that we have such preferences. But certain artificial examples allow such preferences to emerge. Here is an example inspired by Derek Parfit:

> *The Amnesia Case*: I am in hospital for two operations. Both operations are performed without anaesthetic; one lasts for six hours, the other for one hour. I wake up with amnesia. The nurse informs that I have had one operation, and I'm still to have the other. Unfortunately, she doesn't know which operation I had. So all I know is: either (i) I had six hours of pain yesterday and I will have one hour of pain tomorrow or (ii) I had one hour of pain yesterday and I will have six hours of pain tomorrow.[1]

In this example I strongly prefer that (i) be true. Even though, on either scenario, my life will contain those seven hours of pain, I strongly prefer that the six hours of pain be behind me rather than yet to come. I think most people would be of the same opinion.

It might be held that temporally biased attitudes are irrational. All we should care about, it might be said, is that our lives contain as few painful experiences as possible. The distribution of these experiences within one's life is irrelevant. But temporally biased attitudes are so firmly held that this response is implausible. Given that such attitudes are rational, can they be better accounted for on one theory of time rather than the other?

The problem for the B theory

It is hard to see how the B theory can account for such attitudes. According to the B theory, an event's being past or future is simply a matter of it being earlier than the time of speaking or later than the time of speaking. The relations 'earlier than' and 'later than' are perfectly **symmetrical**. There can be no reason for caring more about experiences that are later, rather than earlier, than the time of utterance. That would be as irrational as caring more about the experiences of people to the right of me than about the experiences of people to the left of me (geographically not politically!). My preference for (i) over (ii) is thus irrational, according to the B theory.

Another example illustrates the difficulty facing the B theory:

> *The Gulag*: Ivan Denisovich is sentenced to 25 years hard labour in Siberia. One week into his sentence he is a very unhappy man. One week before his release he is a happy man. But why the difference in attitude? At either time Ivan is only one week from freedom. True, freedom lies one week earlier in the first case and one week later in the second, but why should that make any difference to a B theorist?[2]

It would seem that the B theorist would have to regard Ivan as irrational for having the different attitudes. But this is absurd. Ivan is right to feel depressed at the earlier time and elated at the later time.

The A theory account

Does the A theorist fare any better? On the A theory time has an intrinsic direction, from past to future. As the *now* marches on, past events are moving further and further away from us. That is why it is reasonable to care less about them. Future pains will be experienced, when they are present, and that is why it is reasonable to care more about them. So my attitude in *The Amnesia Case* and Ivan's attitude in *The Gulag* are perfectly rational. It is rational to want the six hours of pain to be behind me because I will then not have to experience them. It is rational for Ivan to be depressed one week into his sentence because the 25 years hard labour are yet to be experienced by him. By the same token, he is right to be elated one week before release because the vast bulk of his punishment is then behind him.

We are not only glad when unpleasant experiences are past rather than future. We are also glad when unpleasant experiences are past rather than present – i.e., when they are no longer present. Arthur Prior once wrote a famous article in which he argued that the B theory could make no sense of the attitude expressed in utterances of 'Thank goodness that's over'.[3] Hugh Mellor reconstructs Prior's argument as follows:

Suppose you have just had a painful experience, e.g., a headache. Now it is over, you say with relief 'Thank goodness that's over.' What are you thanking goodness for? On the face of it, the fact that the headache is no longer a present experience, i.e., is now past. That is presumably why you made your remark after the pain, and not during or before it. Can this ... still be explained [on the B theory]?[4]

Prior's thought is that no B series replacement for 'that's over' can make sense of a 'Thank goodness that's over' utterance. For example, it would be silly to say 'thank goodness the ending of that headache is contemporaneous with this utterance' or 'thank goodness the ending of that headache occurred on 1 January 2013'. Why thank goodness for either of those truths? It always was and always will be true that two events are contemporaneous or that an event ended at a certain time. I could have thanked goodness for those B series facts at any time (had I known about them). The B series surrogates fail to explain why it is appropriate to thank goodness immediately after the headache rather than any other time.

What I am thanking goodness for, it seems, is a tensed or perspectival fact: the fact that the headache, which was present, is now past. Only the A theory, with its **ontology** of shifting **tensed facts**, can make sense of utterances of 'thank goodness that's over'.

A.N. PRIOR (1914–1969)

Arthur Norman Prior was born in New Zealand. He was Professor of Philosophy at Manchester University and later a fellow of Balliol College, Oxford. He died suddenly in 1969, only three years after arriving at Balliol. Prior made major contributions to the development of tense logic and the metaphysics of time. He explored analogies between the logic of necessity and possibility and the logic of past, present and future. The tense operators 'it has been the case that p' and 'it will be the case that p' were held to function analogously to the **modal** operators 'it is necessary that p' and 'it is possible that p'. Thus an ordinary past-tensed sentence such as 'Bill was bald' was thought to be most perspicuously represented as 'it has been the case that: Bill is bald'. Prior thought that tensed propositions were necessary for the expression of temporal facts, and so was an A theorist about time. He often drew on the work of ancient and medieval logicians and was by all accounts an indefatigable and inspiring teacher.

• TIME WITHOUT CHANGE

What is the connection between time and change? It is undeniable that change implies time: change is a temporal process. But does time imply change? That is, is it possible for there to be a period of time during which nothing in the entire universe changes?[4] We are not asking whether there has been or will be such a period of change-free time in our universe. We are asking whether it is metaphysically possible for there to be a period of change-free time. And if it is possible, is it possible for people in such a world to be able to predict when, and for how long, they will undergo a period of change-free time?

The metaphysical question is whether time without change is possible. The epistemic question is whether, if it is possible, matters could be so arranged that people in such a world could know or reasonably believe that a period of change-free time has elapsed. The second question is more important since the bare possibility of time without change would be uninteresting if it were unknowable. Sydney Shoemaker's ingenious paper 'Time without Change' makes a case for answering both questions positively.[5]

Two preliminary points

(i) A theorists hold that time without change is obviously impossible. But that is because they regard the mere passage of time (the moving *now*) as change. However, Shoemaker does not count these A changes, if such there be, as genuine changes. He takes change to be ordinary change, e.g., an object's altering its colour, weight, momentum, etc. So understood, it is an open question whether time involves change.

(ii) It is undeniable that we cannot be aware of a period of change-free time while it is occurring. To be aware of something involves a mental change. So we cannot know that a period of change-free time has elapsed by experiencing it. But that does not mean it is impossible to know whether such a period has elapsed. Perhaps we can know it non-experientially, just as we can only know non-experientially the truth 'at the time of the Big Bang, there were no minds.' We know this truth because of our theoretical knowledge that the conditions at the time of the Big Bang were incompatible with the existence of conscious life. The genius of Shoemaker's example is to show how we might come to have non-experiential knowledge of when, and for how long, there was or will be a period of time without change.

SYDNEY SHOEMAKER (1931 TO PRESENT)

Sydney Shoemaker is a leading American metaphysician and philosopher of mind. He taught for many years at Cornell University, where he received his PhD. His first book *Self-Knowledge and Self-Identity* (1963) is still an excellent introduction to issues concerning the nature and knowledge of the self. It includes his famous brain-transplant argument against the bodily theory of personal identity. Shoemaker pursued these and other themes in his collection of essays *Identity, Cause and Mind* (2nd edn, 2003). In these essays he explored further the nature of first-person knowledge, made vivid the possibility of time without change, defended functionalism about the mind, and proposed a causal theory of properties which implies that the **laws of nature** are necessary rather than **contingent**. He also engaged Richard Swinburne in a debate on personal identity, arguing against Swinburne's Dualist view of persons (*Personal Identity*, Basil Blackwell, 1984).

Shoemaker's world

Shoemaker imagines a possible world divided into three spatial regions: A, B and C. There is typically interaction between the people in all three regions, and people can freely move from one region to the others. But there is the following oddity: every so often one of the regions 'freezes' for a period of one year. Thus, e.g., when A freezes, the people in B and C can see that no events occur in A. When the year is over, everything in A jumps back to life. People in A continue conversations with each other as if no time had elapsed. Of course, things look odd to any A occupant who was looking into B or C prior to the freeze. Just after the end of the freeze, it will appear to such an occupant as if many big changes have occurred instantaneously. What happens to the A region also happens periodically to the other regions, and such freezes are verified by people in the unfrozen regions.

We do not yet have an example of time without change. As we have described this world so far, whenever there is a frozen region, there are always two unfrozen regions in which there is change. However, the more observant members of this world begin to notice a certain regularity to the freezes: A freezes every three years, B freezes every four years, and C freezes every five years. From this information they can work out, assuming the exceptionless character of the three local laws, that every 60 years there is a global freeze: A, B and C are frozen simultaneously for one year. Thus we have a world in which there is, every 60 years, a year of time without any change, and this fact can be known by inhabitants of the world.

Some queries about Shoemaker's world

(i) What causes the end of a freeze? In the case of a local freeze, say in A, it may be events in B or C that cause A's freeze to end. But what causes the end of a global freeze? Not events occurring during the year of global freeze, for there are none. Nor, it might seem, can the cause be any event prior to, or simultaneous with the beginning of, the freeze, for then the freeze would be over as soon as it had begun.

To answer this question we must give up the principle '**no action at a temporal distance**'. That is, the kind of causality at work in our imaginary world must allow 'that an event might be caused directly, and not *via* a mediating causal chain, by an event having occurred a year earlier, or that an event might be caused by such and such's having been the case for a period of one year.'[6] But Shoemaker sees no conceptual problem here. There could be a world, such as the one we are imagining, containing a relation worth calling 'causation', in which there is action at a temporal distance.

(ii) I have occasionally met with the reaction that Shoemaker's world is not an example of time without change because time stops when there is a freeze. But this is not coherent. We can make sense of 'time stopping' in a world only when that world ceases to exist (e.g., as the result of a Big Crunch). If a spatio-temporal universe implodes so that there is literally nothing, then time and space no longer exist. But in no other scenario does it make sense to imagine time grinding to a halt.

A problem for the B theory

The possibility of time without change – which I take Shoemaker to have established – creates a problem for the B theory of time. In a world where there is time without change, time passes while no events occur. But the only sense that a B theorist can make of the 'passage of time' is one event following another in the B series. So if time without change is a possibility, we have an objection to the B theory.

Two responses might be made:

(i)   The present objection goes through if we embrace D. Davidson's conception of events as structureless particulars individuated by their causes and effects (where x is the same event as y **if and only if** x and y have the same causes and same effects).[7]

However, the B theorist could instead endorse J. Kim's property exemplification view of events: an event is an object's exemplifying a property at a time.[8] On this view, events are not always changes. A sphere's being red at some time counts as an event. But it's odd that the B theorist should be forced to accept Kim's view of events, which is anyway implausible. For example, Kim's view implies that Oswald's shooting Kennedy and Oswald's killing Kennedy are distinct events (since the property of shooting is distinct from the property of killing).

(ii) Alternatively, the B theorist may search around for surrogates (in place of events) to stand in B series relations – e.g., moments of time. But it is an empirical question whether time is composed of moments. The B theorist needs it to be a necessary truth that there are moments of time – that in every possible temporal universe there are moments – and it is hard to see how this is to be established.

TIME WITHOUT CHANGE

Many philosophers have thought that time implies change. That is, if time passes, then somewhere in the universe some amount of change, however small, must occur. An A theorist may regard it as obvious that time implies change since the movement of the *now* constitutes change. Others argue for the impossibility of time without change, but only by assuming the implausible premise that time passes only if someone is aware of it passing. We cannot be aware of changeless time, since our continued awareness is itself a change. But perhaps we can have indirect evidence that a period of change-free time has occurred or will do so. Shoemaker's imaginary world nicely illustrates this possibility. By extrapolating from observable regularities, people in his world can predict when a year of time without change will occur.

• TIME TRAVEL

For many, time travel is the most exciting topic in the philosophy of time. From a philosophical point of view, the most fundamental questions about time travel are: is time travel possible, and what would a time-travelling world be like? In asking these questions we are not assuming that time travel has occurred or ever will occur in this world, nor even that time travel is physically possible (i.e., compatible with our laws of nature). We can all enjoy stories and movies involving time travellers, but do such stories represent real metaphysical possibilities? In answering this question I will draw heavily on David Lewis's excellent article 'The Paradoxes of Time Travel'.[9]

Defining 'time travel'

Time travel, says Lewis, '[i]nevitably ... involves a discrepancy between time and time.'[10] Time travel can be to the past or to the future: in either case, the time traveller's journey may have taken an hour, yet he may have ended up hundreds of years into the past or the future. The idea of a discrepancy between time and time may sound incoherent, yet Lewis avoids incoherence:

> by distinguishing time itself, *external time* as I shall call it, from the *personal time* of a particular time traveller: roughly, that which is measured by his wristwatch. His journey takes an hour of personal time, let us say: his wristwatch reads an hour later at arrival than at departure. But the arrival is more than an hour after the departure in external time. ... We may liken intervals of external time to distances as the crow flies, and intervals of personal time to distances along a winding path. The time traveller's life is like a mountain railway. ... [W]e are not dealing here with two independent dimensions. Just as distance along the railway is not a fourth spatial dimension, so a time traveller's personal time is not a second dimension of time.[11]

There is an interesting asymmetry here between past and future. Travel into the future requires a difference in duration between personal time and external time. To take one hour of personal time to travel one hour of external time into the future is not time travel – it is merely continuing to exist. But if I take one hour of personal time to travel one hour of external time into the past, that is time travel. (Homework: what, if anything, does this show about the nature of time?)

Two misconceptions to be avoided

(i) As we understand it, travel into the past involves an individual returning to an earlier time in their own world. A case where a time traveller visits a parallel universe or goes back to a different dimension of time is not time travel. We want to know whether it is possible to travel back through our time, in our world, and befriend luminaries such as Descartes, Hume and Dr Johnson.

(ii) If I travel back in my time machine to 1800, we should not think that there are two 1800s – the initial one which doesn't contain me, and the subsequent one which does. This makes no sense (and may be linked to misconception (i)). There is one and only one 1800 and it either contains me (and always did) or it fails to contain me (and never did).

TIME TRAVEL

Many television shows, movies and science-fiction stories depict an individual travelling in time. What distinguishes a time traveller from an ordinary person is that the personal time of a time traveller differs from external time. A time traveller can travel 1000 years into the past or the future in only one hour of personal time. That is, the time traveller's hair grows the amount it normally does in one hour, his watch tells him that one hour has elapsed, etc. Yet really 1000 years have passed. A time-travelling world is strange indeed. If travel is into the past, it contains backwards causation, and may contain metaphysical oddities, such as **causal loops**. Some think that, if travel into the past is possible, a time traveller who formed the intention to change the past could go back in time and do precisely that. This is the premise of the movie *Terminator*. But this premise is false. No such intention can ever be fulfilled, since 'changing the past' is a contradictory description. There is thus an inconsistency at the very heart of *Terminator*.

• PUZZLES AND PARADOXES

Thus far, we have drawn a distinction between personal time and external time which allows us, *prima facie* at least, to make sense of time travel. However, puzzles and paradoxes may still lurk in the idea of agents travelling in time. These puzzles tend to be presented with respect to travel into the past. In some cases (e.g., backwards causation and causal loops) this is inevitable; in other cases similar puzzles could be posed with respect to travel into the future, but tend not to be for the good reason that we know so little about the future. I agree with Lewis that these puzzles do not present genuine objections to the possibility of time travel. Here are three of the puzzles.

Backwards causation

Time travel into the past necessarily involves backwards causation (with respect to external time). As Lewis says of a traveller into the past: '[y]ou may punch his face before he leaves, causing his eye to blacken centuries ago.'[12] Or again, the time traveller pressing the ignition button in his time machine now causes the time machine to arrive in 1900. Is it an objection to the possibility of travel into the past that it requires backwards causation? Only if the idea of backwards causation, the idea of an effect preceding its cause, is incoherent. However, the 'bilking argument' against backwards causation failed, and we found no theory of causation which is both plausible and rules out backwards causation (see Chapter 7). So we are in no position to object to travel into the past simply on the grounds that it involves backwards causation.

Causal loops

Travel into the past gives rise to the possibility of causal loops. Causal loops are:

> closed causal chains in which some of the causal links are normal in direction and others are reversed. ... Each event on the loop has a causal explanation, being caused by events elsewhere on the loop. This is not to say that the loop as a whole is caused or explicable. It may not be.[13]

A nice example of a causal loop involves the transfer of information. Imagine a time traveller who goes back in time a few years and talks to his earlier self. They discuss time travel, and:

> in the course of the conversation his older self told his younger self how to build a time machine. That information was available in no other way. His older self knew how because his younger self had been told and the information had been preserved [in memory]. His younger self knew, after the conversation, because his older self [had told him]. But where did the information come from in the first place? Why did the whole affair happen? There is simply no answer.[14]

Are causal loops impossible? If they are, then travel into the past must be impossible too. However, there is no reason to think that causal loops are impossible. Many are willing to entertain the possibility of uncaused and inexplicable phenomena: 'God, or the Big Bang, or the entire infinite past of the universe, or the decay of a tritium atom'.[15] If these are possibilities, why not also causal loops? The possibility of causal loops shows that worlds in which people travel into the past are unlike our world, but not that such worlds are impossible.

Grandfather paradox: can a time traveller change the past?

One of the most famous objections to time travel is that a time traveller could change the past. Since it is impossible to change the past, it is concluded that time travel is impossible too.

Changing the past is impossible. To change the past is to make it true that some event that happened didn't happen or to make it true that some event that didn't happen did happen. But it can never be true that some event both happened and didn't happen – not even God can make that true (though Descartes thought otherwise).

There is nothing special about the past in this respect. It is equally impossible to change the present or the future. No one can make it the case that an event happens and does not happen, or that some event will happen and will not happen. Of course, we think we can affect or bring about the future (by choosing to act in certain ways now), but we cannot change it, in the sense just defined.

We must distinguish (i) making the past different from what it was (impossible) from (ii) affecting the past so that it becomes what it was (not obviously impossible). Those who believe that agents can travel into the past commit themselves to the possibility of affecting or bringing about the past. Are they thereby committed to the possibility of a time traveller changing the past?

Lewis thinks not, but begins by outlining the case for thinking that a time traveller can change the past with the following example:

> Consider Tim. He detests his grandfather, whose success in the munitions trade built the family fortune that paid for Tim's time machine. Tim would like nothing so much as to kill Grandfather, but alas he is too late. Grandfather died in his bed in 1957, while Tim was a young boy. But when Tim has built his time machine and travelled to 1920, suddenly he realizes he is not too late after all. He buys a rifle; he spends long hours in target practice; he shadows Grandfather to learn the route of his daily walk.[16]

Tim can kill Grandfather: he has a high-powered rifle; he is a good shot; weather conditions are perfect, etc. Yet Tim cannot kill Grandfather: Grandfather died in his bed in 1957, so he cannot have died in 1920. Consistency demands, despite Tim's best efforts, that he somehow fail to kill Grandfather. Why does he fail? 'For some commonplace reason. Perhaps some noise distracts him at the last moment, perhaps he misses despite all his target practice, perhaps his nerve fails, perhaps he even feels a pang of unaccustomed mercy.'[17] Hence, concludes Lewis, it is wrong to think that a time traveller can change the past.

Comments on Lewis's solution

(i)   It may be thought that Lewis has just replaced one contradiction with another. Has the contradiction 'Grandfather dies in 1920 and in 1957' not been replaced by the contradiction 'Tim both can and cannot kill Grandfather'? In which case, travel into the past still implies a contradiction.

Lewis has a nice reply to this objection. There is no contradiction since 'can' is equivocal. Can I speak Finnish? Yes and no. Relative to facts about the structure of my larynx and nervous system, yes I can. But relative to the fact that I have never learnt Finnish, no I can't. Similarly, relative to one set of facts, Tim can kill Grandfather (e.g., facts about Tim's rifle, his shooting ability, the weather conditions, and so on). But relative to another, more inclusive, set of facts (including the fact that Grandfather was not killed in 1920), Tim cannot kill

Grandfather. There would only be a contradiction if Tim can and cannot kill Grandfather, relative to the same set of facts. But that is not something to which a defender of time travel is committed.

(ii) Tim's attempt is causally self-undermining: he is trying to eliminate one of the causes of his own existence. This makes Tim's attempt doubly impossible. It is self-undermining as well as an attempt to change the past. But the self-undermining aspect is inessential to Lewis's solution. Even if Tim tried to assassinate Grandfather's partner, he would also fail, for the same type of reason (given that, e.g., the partner lived until 1950).

(iii) Lewis is right that Tim's story, if consistent, must continue along the lines he suggests. Somehow Tim fails: his gun jams; he shoots someone else by mistake; he faints, etc. This is true however many attempts he makes. But there is something odd about this. Tim is unable to do something – shoot someone – which by all ordinary criteria he is able to do. Ordinarily, we don't regard the fact that someone will not succeed in doing something as a constraint on his ability to do it. If I truly predict that Phil 'The Power' Taylor will not hit bullseye, we don't think that that truth affected his ability to hit bullseye.

But if Tim had his wits about him, he would realize that the fact that Grandfather lived until 1957 does affect his ability to kill Grandfather in 1920. The oddity of Tim's situation is that he ought to take a fatalistic attitude to his inability to kill Grandfather in 1920 (in light of his knowledge that Grandfather was not killed in 1920), even though he is, in general, able to kill people by shooting them. But none of this shows travel into the past to be impossible.

• TIME TRAVEL AND THEORIES OF TIME

How does time travel fare on the theories of time discussed in the previous chapter? (i) If Presentism is true, and only the present is real, time travel is impossible. If past and future are both unreal, there is no time for the traveller to visit. (ii) If the Growing Universe View is true – past and present real, future unreal – travel into the future is impossible. Yet travel into the past, indeed any form of backwards causation, ought to be impossible too. If I travel back to 1900 I would have come from the future. Yet the future is unreal according to the Growing Universe View. (This is symptomatic of an incoherence in the Growing Universe View.) (iii) Only the B theory, which holds that past, present and future are equally real, allows for travel into both the past and the future.

• CONCLUDING REMARKS

We have looked at three puzzles about time – temporally biased attitudes, time without change and time travel – and we have arrived at some interesting conclusions. The existence of temporally biased attitudes, and the possibility of time without change, both yield problems for the B theory. Our discussion of time travel concluded that a world in which time travel occurs is very different from our world, but possible nonetheless.

• STUDY QUESTIONS

- Could the B theorist reasonably claim that our temporally biased attitudes are irrational?
- Can the A theorist explain satisfactorily why we care more about future experiences than about past ones?
- Does Shoemaker's imaginary world pose a problem for the B theory?
- Are there any genuine paradoxes of time travel?
- Could a time traveller be his own father? How?

• ANNOTATED FURTHER READING

R. Hanley, 'No End in Sight: Causal loops in philosophy, physics and fiction', *Synthese*, Vol. 141 (2004), pp. 123–52. Some interesting reflections on causal loops.

P. Horwich, *Asymmetries in Time* (Cambridge, Mass.: MIT Press, 1987), Chapter 7. A useful, if technical, discussion of Kurt Gödel's solution to the Einstein field equations. Gödel's solution allows for travel into the past.

D. Lewis, 'The Paradoxes of Time Travel', American *Philosophical Quarterly*, Vol. 13, No. 1, 1976. Reprinted in his *Philosophical Papers*, Vol. II (Oxford: Oxford University Press, 1986), Chapter 18. The classic philosophical treatment of time travel. Lewis's article is very readable, and free of technicality.

H. Mellor, *Real Time* (Cambridge: Cambridge University Press, 1985). The most sustained defence of the B theory available, containing a response to Prior's 'Thank Goodness That's Over' argument.

A.N. Prior, 'Thank Goodness That's Over', *Philosophy*, Vol. 34 (1959), pp. 12–17. Clear statement of a much-discussed problem for the B theory.

S. Shoemaker, 'Time without Change', in his *Identity, Cause and Mind* (Cambridge: Cambridge University Press, 2003), 2nd edn, pp. 49–67. A clear and thorough presentation of the case for the possibility of time without change.

R. Le Poidevin and M. MacBeath (eds), *The Philosophy of Time* (Oxford: Oxford University Press, 1993). A useful collection containing many of the articles discussed here.

• INTERNET RESOURCES

B. Jack Copeland, 'Arthur Prior', *The Stanford Encyclopedia of Philosophy* (Fall 2008 Edition), ed. Edward N. Zalta, URL = <http://plato.stanford.edu/archives/fall2008/entries/prior/>.

P. Horwich (1998), 'Time Travel', *Routledge Encyclopedia of Philosophy*, ed. E. Craig. Retrieved 31 May 2006 from <http://www.rep.routledge.com/article/Q108>.

F. Arntzenius and T. Maudlin (2005), 'Time Travel and Modern Physics', *The Stanford Encyclopedia of Philosophy* (Summer 2005 edition), ed. Edward N. Zalta. Retrieved 31 May 2006 from <http://plato.stanford.edu/archives/sum2005/entries/time-travel-phys>.

• NOTES

1. See D. Parfit, *Reasons and Persons* (Oxford: Oxford University Press, 1984), pp. 165–6.
2. G. Schlesinger, *Metaphysics* (Oxford: Blackwell, 1983), p. 109.
3. A.N. Prior, 'Thank Goodness That's Over', *Philosophy*, Vol. 34 (1959), pp. 12–17.
4. H. Mellor, *Real Time* (Cambridge: Cambridge University Press, 1985), p. 48.
5. S. Shoemaker, 'Time without Change', in his *Identity, Cause and Mind* (Cambridge: Cambridge University Press, 1984), pp. 49–67.
6. *Ibid.*, p. 62.
7. D. Davidson, 'The Individuation of Events', in *Essays on Actions and Events* (Oxford: Clarendon Press, 2001), 2nd edn.
8. See J. Kim, 'Events as Property Exemplifications', in his *Supervenience and Mind* (Cambridge, Cambridge University Press, 1993).
9. D. Lewis, 'The Paradoxes of Time Travel', *American Philosophical Quarterly*, Vol. 13, No. 1 (1976), pp. 145–52.
10. *Ibid.*, p. 145.
11. *Ibid.*, pp. 146–7.
12. *Ibid.*, p. 148.
13. *Ibid.*, pp. 148–9.
14. *Ibid.*, p. 149.
15. *Ibid.*, p. 149.
16. *Ibid.*, p. 149.
17. *Ibid.*, p. 150.

10
·free will

• INTRODUCTION

In this chapter we will be concerned with two broad lines of attack on the thesis that we have free will. It may appear outrageous to attack this thesis, since it seems to us that we act freely virtually all the time. Indeed, it may be that self-conscious rational agents must believe they are free in order to act at all. However, since the beginning of philosophy, our free will has been called into question.

The first line of attack on free will stems from various arguments of the fatalist. The most famous of these is Aristotle's 'sea-battle' argument, which rests on the assumption that there are truths about the future. We examine two ways of responding to Aristotle's reasoning. In addition, Michael Dummett outlines a different fatalist argument, and suggests that, if the fatalist's reasoning is faulty, so is the line of reasoning which attempts to show that it is always irrational to attempt to influence the past.

The other line of attack emerges from the worry that free will cannot flourish in a deterministic setting, nor in an **indeterministic** one. If this were right, then free will would be impossible. Indeed, Galen Strawson has recently argued that free will is a logically unsatisfiable, hence incoherent, concept. This second line of attack is more worrying than the first.

The issue of free will is important, not just as an issue in metaphysics, but also because it is generally assumed that moral responsibility requires free will. Hence, if free will is an illusion, so too is moral responsibility, thereby undermining those social, moral and legal practices that presuppose such responsibility. It would be hard to overestimate the revisionary effect on our conception of ourselves and others if we thought free will and moral responsibility illusory.

• FATALISM

The conclusion of fatalist reasoning, as its name suggests, is that we are prisoners of fate: we cannot do anything other than we actually do. The classic argument for fatalism is give by Aristotle in *De Interpretatione*.[1] Here is a presentation of the argument. The premises and conclusion are intended to be *a priori*, necessary truths, and 'inevitable' means 'outwith any human control or influence':

(1) Either there will be a sea-battle tomorrow or there will not be a sea-battle tomorrow.

(2) If there will be a sea-battle tomorrow, then it's inevitable that there will be a sea-battle tomorrow.

(3) If there will not be a sea-battle tomorrow, then it's inevitable that there will not be a sea-battle tomorrow.

(4) Hence, it is either inevitable that there will be a sea-battle tomorrow or inevitable that there will not be a sea-battle tomorrow.

(5) Hence, since there is nothing special about sea-battles or tomorrow, whatever happens at any future time is inevitable.

A theory response

How we respond to this argument will depend on which theory of time we accept: A theory or B theory. A theorists accept the so-called 'Aristotelian solution': denying (1).

If the future is unreal, there is no future fact to make true either 'there will be a sea-battle tomorrow' or 'there will not be a sea-battle tomorrow'. Since a disjunction cannot be true if neither disjunct is true, (1) is not true. In denying (1), the A theorist denies the universal validity of the Law of Excluded Middle – the law which holds that, for all propositions p, either p or not-p.

B theory response

How should the B theorist respond? Since the B theorist holds that the future is real, he cannot deny (1). Since the argument is clearly valid – from (1) – (3), (4) and (5) follow – the B theorist must deny premises (2) and (3). And why not? After all, (2) and (3) seem far from mandatory. Why should truth imply inevitability? Intuitively, it's true that I will have eggs for breakfast tomorrow, but not inevitable. Knowing well my own gastronomic intentions, I know that I will have eggs tomorrow. But that will be the result of my free choice.

However, matters are not so simple. Consider the following argument. As above, premises and conclusion are intended to be *a priori*, necessary truths, and 'inevitable' means 'outwith any human control or influence':

(6) Either there was a sea-battle yesterday or there was not a sea-battle yesterday.

(7) If there was a sea-battle yesterday, then it's inevitable that there was a sea-battle yesterday.

(8) If there was not a sea-battle yesterday, then it's inevitable that there was not a sea-battle yesterday.

(9) Hence, it is either inevitable that there was a sea-battle yesterday or inevitable that there was not a sea-battle yesterday.

Many B theorists (amongst others) will regard the (6) – (9) argument as unexceptional and non-paradoxical. It is a commonplace that the past is fixed and determinate. But how can an (anti-fatalist) B theorist endorse the (6) – (9) argument yet criticize the (1) – (5) argument? If backwards causation is impossible, this question is easy to answer. The impossibility of backwards causation would immediately underwrite the truth of (7) and (8).

However, we have discovered no theory of causation which is both plausible and precludes backwards causation. Nor is the standard bilking argument against backwards causation persuasive. (See Chapter 7.) Granted the **metaphysical possibility** of backwards causation, the only difference between the two arguments is the tenses, and that cannot be a relevant difference for the B theorist.[2] The (anti-fatalist) B theorist must therefore be critical of both Aristotle's argument and the (6) – (9) argument.

The only option for the B theorist is to hold that (7) and (8) are not necessary truths. To hold this is not to embrace the incoherent idea that the past can be changed. Nor is it to embrace the idea that the past might be fuzzy or indeterminate – 'waiting' to be determined by present or future actions. In any possible world, there is one and only one past and any event either happened at some past time or it did not.

To deny the inevitability of the past is to embrace the idea that the past is not fixed; that is, it is metaphysically possible to act now so as to make the past be what it was. Had our world contained suitable backwards causal chains, it could be true that there was a sea-battle yesterday precisely because of my present actions. The past is not, in virtue of its nature or essence, fixed. The B theorist can avoid fatalism, but only if the idea of influencing or bringing about the past is coherent.

FATALISM

The classic fatalist argument is presented by Aristotle in Chapter 9 of his *De Interpretatione*. Either there will be a sea-battle tomorrow or there won't. It seems to follow that, whichever is true, it is true of necessity. The necessity here is not logical necessity, but inevitability. If sound, this argument generalizes to all future human actions, implying that we are fated to do whatever we do. The A theorist has a simple response: since the future is unreal, there are no truths about the future. Hence, Aristotle's argument does not get off the ground. Fatalism is more of a problem for the B theorist. The B theorist can reply to Aristotle's reasoning but only by denying the widely held belief that the past is, of necessity, fixed. The B theorist must argue that it is possible (in worlds containing suitable backwards causal chains) for rational agents to influence the past, to help make the past be what it was.

Bringing about the past

But is the idea coherent? One of the most illuminating discussions is to be found in Michael Dummett's excellent article 'Bringing about the Past'.[3] Dummett finds no contradiction in the idea of backwards causation, or in the idea of observing such causation. But matters are more complicated when we imagine agents in such a world, aware of backward causal connections, and forming the intention to do something now to cause something to have happened earlier.

One model is retrospective prayer. A father, unaware of his son's fate, prays to God to make it the case that his son not have drowned in a ship known to have gone down a few hours previously. But this is a special case. We are, says Dummett, relying on the idea that God knew (in advance) of the father's prayer and, as a result, intervened to save the son.

Dummett then moves to a non-theological example. He imagines a certain tribe, whose young men regularly go into battle. The villagers notice a certain odd correlation. Whenever the chief dances after the battle, but before the men return home, the men fought bravely. When the chief fails to dance, they always discover that the men did not acquit themselves bravely. The chief believes that his dancing helped to bring it about that the men fought bravely. Can we convict the chief of irrationality?

The chief's case that he caused the young men to have been brave rests on two assumptions: (i) that there was a positive correlation between his dancing and the young men's bravery; and (ii) that the dancing was in his power to do as he chose. We are to imagine that the circumstances turn out to be favourable to both assumptions. Whenever he danced the men were brave; whenever he failed to dance the men were cowardly. Never did he find himself unable to dance when he chose to. (Assumption (ii) is important – without it one might conclude that the men's bravery caused the chief's dancing.)

But there is a complicating factor. If the chief were to be told, after a battle but before his dancing, that the young men were brave, he would clearly have no reason to dance. If the chief knew that the men had acted bravely, it would be irrational for him to dance. Indeed the mere possibility that he might know, through a third party, whether the men had been brave or not, would seem to compromise the rationality of his dancing.

So the chief must assume: (iii) prior to his dancing, it is not possible for him to know, independently of his intention to dance, whether the men were brave. This is an instance of a principle we accept for one kind of knowledge (or justified belief) about the future. For example, in the normal course of events, I do not know that I will have eggs for breakfast independently of my knowledge of my present intention to eat eggs tomorrow morning. The chief must assume that an analogous principle applies to knowledge of past events we bring about.

Some philosophers hold that this principle cannot be right, that all past truths must be in principle knowable, whatever one's present intentions.[4] Dummett concedes that (iii) is difficult for us to accept, but concludes that we could not convict the chief of irrationality if he stuck to (i) – (iii), and all the evidence was favourable. In which case, the idea of bringing about the past is not an irrational or incoherent one. The B theorist can make use of this idea in criticizing premises (7) and (8).

Dummett's fatalist argument

Dummett imagines a response to the chief along the following lines:

> Either the men have been brave or they have not. If they have, your dancing will be superfluous. If they have not, your dancing will be not be effective. So in either case your dancing is pointless: it cannot make any difference to whether they have been brave or not.

Dummett points out that this is the exact analogue of a familiar fatalist argument:

> The standard form of the fatalist argument was very popular in London during the bombing. The siren sounds, and I set off for the air-raid shelter in order to avoid being killed by a bomb. The fatalist argues, 'Either you are going to be killed by a bomb or you are not going to be. If you are, then any precautions you take will be ineffective. If you are not, all precautions you take are superfluous. Therefore, it is pointless to take precautions.'[5]

If we are critical of this fatalist argument, we should be equally critical of the just mooted response to the chief.

We can write the fatalist argument explicitly as follows:

(10) Either you are going to be killed by a bomb or you are not going to be killed by a bomb.

(11) If you are going to be killed by a bomb, any precautions you take will be ineffective.

(12) If you are not going to be killed by a bomb, any precautions you take will be superfluous.

So:

(13) It is pointless to take precautions.

The A theorist will reject (10). But Dummett wants to criticize the argument as a B theorist would, so that he can then make the same response to the analogous argument against the chief. The diagnosis is not difficult: we have no reason to accept (12). Premise (12) is not guaranteed to be true: it may be that you are not killed by a bomb precisely because you took precautions. In that case the precautions you took were not superfluous. If Dummett is right, the chief can make exactly the analogous response: 'it's not true that if the men have been brave, my dancing will be superfluous. On the contrary, they fought bravely precisely because I danced.'

In sum: the A theorist has a simple response to both Aristotle's 'sea-battle' argument and to Dummett's fatalist argument. The B theorist also has responses to both arguments. But, in replying to those arguments, the B theorist incurs a commitment to the possibility of the **open past**, the possibility (circumstances permitting) that we can influence the past as we do the future.

THOMAS HOBBES (1588–1679)

Hobbes is best known as a political philosopher. In his book *Leviathan*, published in 1651, he argued for rule by an absolute sovereign as a bulwark against civil disorder. Hobbes attempted to show how politics could be a science. His account of the nature of matter was the foundation for his theory of human psychology, which in turn provided the foundation for his theory of politics. For Hobbes, the entire universe, including human thought and behaviour, is just matter in motion. All causation is mechanistic and necessary: everything is necessitated by what has gone before. Nonetheless, Hobbes held his mechanistic view of the universe to be consistent with the existence of God (conceived as a material being), with conscious mental states (also conceived as physical), and with human freedom. Hobbes was thus one of the first compatibilists: 'Liberty and Necessity are consistent,' he wrote. '[T]he actions which men voluntarily do ... proceed from liberty, and because every act of man's will ... proceeds from some cause, and that from another cause, in a continual chain, [such voluntary actions] proceed from necessity' (*Leviathan*).

• FREE WILL AND DETERMINISM

Fatalism is not the only threat to free action. Since the time of Thomas Hobbes (1588–1679), philosophers have worried that determinism threatens free will. Some – the compatibilists (such as Hobbes and David Hume) – regard the tension as illusory and hold that free will and determinism are compatible. Indeed, some compatibilists hold that free will requires the truth of determinism.

Others – the incompatibilists – hold that the tension is real enough: free will and determinism are incompatible. However, incompatibilists then divide into two camps: the libertarians, who conclude that, since we are free, determinism must be false; and the hard determinists, who conclude that, since determinism is true, we lack free will.

Finally, there are those philosophers (such as Galen Strawson) who hold that the truth or otherwise of determinism is irrelevant to whether we have free will. The concept of free will is internally incoherent, and can be shown to be so on purely *a priori* grounds. Hence free will is an illusion. Since moral responsibility presupposes free will, moral responsibility is an illusion too.

FREE WILL AND DETERMINISM

The thesis of determinism has traditionally been thought to threaten freedom of thought and action. If determinism is true then, given the **laws of nature** and the state of the universe at any arbitrary past time, it is determined that you read these words now. Compatibilists hold that determinism does not compromise our freedom. Libertarians hold that it does, and conclude that, since we are free, determinism is false. But is it not for science to tell us whether determinism is true? Anyway, how can indeterminism provide a congenial home for free will? Carefully reasoned decisions leading to predictable actions hardly seem to involve indeterministic or random happenings. Others hold that compatibilists and libertarians are both wrong. Freedom is incompatible with determinism and with indeterminism. That is, free will is logically impossible. I cannot be the 'final root of all my determinations' in the way required by the concept of free will. Ascriptions of moral responsibility, in as much as they presuppose free will, are without foundation.

Two definitions of free action

Assessment of this debate is complicated by the fact that the two defenders of free will – compatibilist and libertarian – offer quite different definitions of what is it to act freely. According to the compatibilist:

(CFW) X acts freely **if and only if** X's action is caused by X's beliefs and desires.

Thus if I wave to a friend my action is free provided it was brought about by my belief that that person is my friend and my desire to greet him.

According to the libertarian:

(LFW) X acts freely if and only if X could have acted other than he did.

On this view, if I wave to a friend my action is free provided I could have refrained from waving (the past and laws of nature remaining the same). Compatibilist free will is, of course, compatible with determinism; libertarian free will is inconsistent with determinism.

Determinism defined

Determinism is the thesis that, given the laws of nature, and the state of the universe at any time t, it is impossible for the history of the universe (before and after t) to be other than it is. Alternatively, it can be rendered as the thesis that every event has a cause, where causes are understood to necessitate or determine their effects.

If the universe is deterministic, the past, together with the laws of nature, uniquely determine the future. The actual future is the only possible future. The regularities we observe around us, from the motion of the planets to more mundane terrestrial regularities, support the claim that our universe is deterministic.

Both compatibilist and libertarian accounts of free will are *prima facie* plausible. But both face problems.

Compatibilist free will

According to compatibilists, free action is to be contrasted, not with universal causation or determinism, but with constraints of various familiar kinds. We say that someone is unfree only when they are suffering from kleptomania, brainwashed, handcuffed or suchlike. It is the presence of such specific constraints that robs a person of their freedom, not the truth of determinism.

An ingenious **thought-experiment** devised by Harry Frankfurt supports the compatibilist view.[6] Here is a simple version of his thought-experiment. Suppose that Smith plans to rob his local bank. He waits until nightfall, then duly executes his plan. In terms of the actual course of events this is like any other bank robbery, except for one detail. Unbeknownst to Smith, an evil, robbery-loving demon has been monitoring Smith's brain and was prepared to intervene if Smith had shown any hesitation about committing the robbery. If Smith had attempted to change his mind, he would have found himself unable to do so. As it happens, Smith wanted the money and didn't change his mind, so the demon never had to intervene in the actual course of Smith's life.

We have a robust intuition that Smith's action of robbing the bank was free, and one for which he was fully morally responsible. The planning and execution of the robbery were entirely due to Smith. The demon did not cause Smith to do anything. Yet Smith could not have done otherwise: in respect of the robbery, he could not have chosen or acted differently. Doesn't this show that free will does not require the ability to do otherwise, and so is compatible with determinism?

Not necessarily. Smith's beliefs and desires caused his action of robbing of the bank. But those beliefs and desires were themselves caused by previous beliefs and desires, which were themselves caused by previous events, and so on, stretching back to events before Smith was born. If determinism is true, Smith could not but have had the beliefs and desires he does have. Viewed this way, Smith no longer seems a free agent. His beliefs and desires seem to be merely events that occur 'in' him, over which he has no more control than he does over the motion of the planets. What holds for Smith, of course, holds for us all – if determinism is true. Our intuition that Smith acted freely in robbing the bank depended on our implicit assumption that Smith was acting on his 'own' beliefs and desires. That is what has been questioned. Consequently, determinism does not seem compatible with free action.

Libertarian free will

The libertarian agrees with the just mooted line of reasoning, and takes it to show that free will and determinism are indeed incompatible. Since we evidently have free will, the libertarian concludes that our universe is indeterministic. Free action is possible only in indeterministic universes.

Here are two problems with this argument:

(i)   The libertarian's reasoning is hostage to empirical fortune. It is an empirical question whether determinism is true. Many physicists currently think that our universe is indeterministic, at least at the sub-atomic level. But that may not be the considered opinion of future physicists. If it turned out that the universe is deterministic, the libertarian position would collapse into that of the hard determinist. Then free will would be an illusion.

(ii) It has seemed to many that an indeterministic universe does not provide an hospitable environment for free will. Consider a rational agent carefully deliberating over some important moral question and then deciding upon what he takes to be the right course of action. Random or indeterministic happenings have no role to play here. If anything, they would undermine the legitimacy of the process of reasoning. An agent could hardly be held responsible for an action that resulted from a random happening over which they had no control. It would be mere good luck if they did the right thing.

Free will and the self

It is important to note that none of the objections to compatibilist and libertarian free will presupposes any particular conception of ourselves. Whether or not we are immaterial souls, if our actions are brought about in a deterministic way, the objections to compatibilism still apply; if not, the objections to libertarianism still apply. **Dualism** provides no better refuge for free will than **Physicalism**.

GALEN STRAWSON (1952 TO PRESENT)

Galen Strawson, son of the late Oxford philosopher P.F. Strawson, is currently a professor of philosophy at the University of Reading. He was educated at Cambridge, Oxford and the Sorbonne, and he previously taught at Oxford and the City University of New York Graduate School. A creative, rigorous and independent thinker, Strawson has produced a number of important books to date. In 1986 he published *Freedom and Belief* in which he argued that free will and ultimate moral responsibility are incoherent notions. Free will is an illusion. In 1989 he published *The Secret Connexion* in which he argued that Hume did not hold a regularity theory of causation and believed in natural necessity.

In 1995 he published *Mental Reality* and argued therein that conscious experience is the distinctive mark of the mental and that there is no conceptual connection between a subject's possession of mental states and his behaviour or dispositions to behaviour. He called his view a 'naturalized Cartesianism'. More recently, Strawson has published on the nature of the self – *Selves: An Essay in Revisionary Metaphysics* (2009).

• IS THE NOTION OF FREE WILL INCOHERENT?

Neither the compatibilist nor the libertarian account of free will is acceptable. The fault may lie with the very idea of free will. Galen Strawson has recently argued that, independently of considerations to do with determinism and indeterminism, the notion of free will is incoherent.[7] Free will and moral responsibility require a conception of self-determination which is logically unsatisfiable. J.G. Fichte (1762–1814) nicely captured this paradoxical notion of self-determination:

> What I desired was this: that I myself, that of which I am conscious as my own being and person, ... that this 'I' would be independent, would be something which exists not by another or through another, but of myself, and, as such, would be the final root of all my determinations.[8]

Why think self-determination impossible? Strawson's thought is that self-determination requires you to be ultimately responsible for what you do. To be ultimately responsible for what you do, you must be ultimately responsible for what you are in some mental respects (e.g., character). But it is impossible to be ultimately responsible for the way you are in mental respects (or in any other respect). For this would require that you intentionally brought it about that you had a certain mental nature. But this in turn would require that you had a prior mental nature, which in turn would require a prior mental nature which ... and so on, *ad infinitum*.

Hence, on pain of a **vicious regress**, it is impossible to be ultimately responsible for the way you are in any mental respect, and so it is impossible to be ultimately responsible for what you do. In the absence of such responsibility there can be no self-determination and hence no freedom.

Just as nothing can cause itself to exist (since, in order to do so, it would already have to exist) so no person can be ultimately responsible for their mental nature. Strawson's challenge to defenders of free will is to either (i) construct a notion of free will worth having which does not require self-determination or (ii) show that self-determination is not, after all, an impossible concept.

• CONCLUDING REMARKS

We have examined the two best-known attacks on human freedom: fatalism and determinism. We looked at two versions of the fatalist argument (Aristotle's and Dummett's). The A theorist has an easy reply to both versions. The B theorist can reply to both versions, but his response succeeds only if there is no incoherence in the idea of an agent bringing about the past.

A bigger threat to free will stems from the serious difficulties facing compatibilist and libertarian conceptions of free will. These difficulties, in turn, may flow from the logically unsatisfiable character of our notions of free will and moral responsibility, as Galen Strawson has forcefully argued.

• STUDY QUESTIONS

- Outline Aristotle's 'sea-battle' argument for fatalism.
- Can the B theorist respond adequately to Aristotle's argument?
- What would it be for the past to be open?
- Is either of the compatibilist or libertarian positions defensible?
- Is the notion of free will self-undermining?

• ANNOTATED FURTHER READING

A.J. Ayer, 'Fatalism', in his *The Concept of a Person* (London: Macmillan, 1963), pp. 235–69. A clear and no-nonsense critique of standard fatalist reasoning.

A.J. Ayer, 'Freedom and Necessity', in his *Philosophical Essays* (London: Macmillan, 1965), pp. 271–85. A modern defence of compatibilism about free will.

R. Clarke, *Libertarian Accounts of Free Will* (Oxford: Oxford University Press, 2003). A thorough overview of libertarian attempts to make sense of free will.

M. Dummett, 'Bringing about the Past', in his *Truth and Other Enigmas* (Cambridge, Mass.: Harvard University Press, 1978), pp. 333–51. A classic, but difficult, discussion of whether it can ever be rational to attempt to affect the past with, *en route*, a comparison with, and diagnosis of, one fatalist argument.

G. Strawson, *Freedom and Belief* (Oxford: Oxford University Press, 1986). A clear and readable defence of the radical view that free will and moral responsibility are illusions.

P.F. Strawson, 'Freedom and Resentment', in his *Freedom and Resentment and Other Essays* (London: Methuen, 1974), pp. 1–26. A very influential article in which P.F. Strawson attempts to show that ascriptions of freedom and moral responsibility can be neither supported nor overturned by the truth or otherwise of determinism.

P. van Inwagen, *An Essay on Free Will* (Oxford: Clarendon Press, 1983). A clear and thorough defence of incompatibilism, with a useful discussion of fatalism.

G. Watson, *Free Will* (Oxford: Oxford University Press, 2003). A useful collection of the best work on free will in the past half-century.

• INTERNET RESOURCES

E. Craig (1998), 'Fatalism', *Routledge Encyclopedia of Philosophy*, ed. E. Craig. Retrieved 31 May 2006 from <http://www.rep.routledge.com/article/N096>.

J. Maier, 'Abilities', *The Stanford Encyclopedia of Philosophy* (Spring 2010 Edition), ed. Edward N. Zalta, URL = <http://plato.stanford.edu/archives/spr2010/entries/abilities/>.

M. McKenna (2004), 'Compatibilism', *The Stanford Encyclopedia of Philosophy* (Summer 2004 edition), ed. Edward N. Zalta. Retrieved 31 May 2006 from <http://plato. stanford.edu/archives/sum2004/entries/compatibilism>.

T. O'Connor (2005), 'Free Will', *The Stanford Encyclopedia of Philosophy* (Summer 2005 edition), ed. Edward N. Zalta. Retrieved 31 May 2006 from <http://plato. stanford. edu/archives/sum2005/entries/freewill>.

H. Rice (2006), 'Fatalism', *The Stanford Encyclopedia of Philosophy* (Winter 2002 edition), ed. Edward N. Zalta. Retrieved 31 May 2006 from <http://plato.stanford. edu/archives/win2002/entries/fatalism>.

G. Strawson (1998, 2004), 'Free will', *Routledge Encyclopedia of Philosophy*, ed. E. Craig. Retrieved 31 May 2006 from<http://www.rep.routledge.com/article/V014>.

L. Zagzebski (2005), 'Foreknowledge and Free Will', *The Stanford Encyclopedia of Philosophy* (Fall 2005 edition), ed. Edward N. Zalta. Retrieved 31 May 2006 from <http://plato. stanford.edu/archives/fall2005/entries/free-will-foreknowledge>.

• NOTES

1. *De interpretatione*, ed. C.W.A. Whitaker (Oxford: Oxford University Press, 2002), Book 9, sections 18a–19b.
2. D.H. Mellor is a B theorist who denies the possibility of backwards causation – see his *Real Time* (Cambridge: Cambridge University Press, 1981). His argument against backwards causation is complex and open to various objections. For useful discussion see Faye, Jan, 'Backward Causation', *The Stanford Encyclopedia of Philosophy* (Spring 2010 Edition), ed. Edward N. Zalta, URL = <http://plato. stanford.edu/archives/spr2010/entries/causation-backwards/>.
3. M. Dummett, 'Bringing about the Past', in his *Truth and Other Enigmas* (Cambridge, Mass.: Harvard University Press, 1978).
4. For example, see H. Mellor, *Real Time* (Cambridge: Cambridge University Press, 1981), p. 183.
5. Dummett, *op. cit.*, p. 339.
6. H. Frankfurt, 'Moral Responsibility and Alternate Possibilities', *Journal of Philosophy*, Vol. 66 (1969), pp. 829–39.
7. G. Strawson, *Freedom and Belief* (Oxford: Oxford University Press, 1986). See also his 'The Impossibility of Moral Responsibility', *Philosophical Studies*, Vol. 75 (1994), pp. 5–24.
8. J.G. Fichte, *The Vocation of Man*, ed. R. Chisholm (New York: The Liberal Arts Press, 1956), p. 27.

11

·facts

• INTRODUCTION

Some philosophers are suspicious of facts; other philosophers embrace them. The latter philosophers think of the world as structured into facts, in virtue of which our sentences or propositions are true. These theorists assume a meaty or substantial conception of facts. That is, they do not regard 'it is a fact that P' as merely a more emphatic way of saying 'it is true that P'. In addition, some theorists (e.g., Wittgenstein and Armstrong) regard facts as the fundamental units of being, prior to objects and properties.

Facts, on any substantial conception, are worldly, non-linguistic entities (e.g., Fred's being fat) which stand in opposition to sentences, statements, propositions or beliefs. Sentences, propositions, etc. represent; facts are what are represented.

Facts can be **concrete** or **abstract**. On some theories, facts are the obtaining of states of affairs, where states of affairs consist of combinations of objects. (This was the view of the early Wittgenstein.) On other theories, facts consist in the instantiation of properties and relations in objects (e.g., the table's being square). On such theories, facts are typically understood as 'additions to being', not reducible to objects, properties and relations. (This is David Armstrong's view.) For example, Bill's hating Mary and Mary's hating Bill are distinct facts, yet involve the very same objects and relations.

In this chapter we will look at two theories – Wittgenstein's **Logical Atomism** (a classic example of the correspondence theory of truth, discussed further in the next chapter) and Armstrong's truthmaker theory – both of which commit themselves to facts.

LUDWIG WITTGENSTEIN (1889–1951)

Ludwig Wittgenstein was born into a large and wealthy family in Vienna in 1889. He enrolled to study with Bertrand Russell in Cambridge, and the two soon entered into a vigorous and combative relationship. Wittgenstein came from a family with a history of mental instability, and was himself of a remarkably intense disposition. His experiences in the trenches during the First World War may have unhinged him even further. His first book and eventual PhD thesis – the highly obscure and mystical *Tractatus Logico-Philosophicus* – was published in 1921. Having claimed to have solved all the problems of philosophy, Wittgenstein went off to be an architect and school teacher. In the late 1920s and early 1930s Wittgenstein realized that he had not solved all the problems of philosophy, and embarked on a voluminous series of original and penetrating writings on many areas of philosophy, especially the philosophy of language, mind and mathematics. His posthumously published *Philosophical Investigations* (1953) is the clearest expression of his later approach to philosophy. He died in Cambridge in 1951.

• WITTGENSTEIN'S LOGICAL ATOMISM

Wittgenstein's Logical Atomism is contained in his *Tractatus Logico-Philosophicus* (1922).[1] The *Tractatus* is written in a series of short, numbered paragraphs. It contains no explicitly formulated arguments, and is probably the most compressed work of philosophy ever produced. It is ultimately a mystical tract, a ladder to be kicked away in order that we may 'see the world aright' (6.54).

The treatise is somewhat compromised by the fact that it fails to meet its own standards for meaningfulness. Though this consequence would have daunted a lesser man, Wittgenstein took it in his stride and, indeed, appeared to embrace it. The work seems to have had a cathartic effect on Wittgenstein. Having cleansed himself of the desire to philosophise, he promptly gave up philosophy and became (without much success) a school teacher. A few years later, in the late 1920s, he returned to philosophy.

If we read the *Tractatus* as a straight work of philosophy, its main ideas are the following. There is a **structural isomorphism** (identity of form) between language and reality, and this isomorphism is necessary for language to represent or be about reality. Since language does represent reality, we can know ***a priori*** that language and reality share the same form.

Language, at its fully analysed level, is composed of elementary propositions, which are composed only of names. Elementary propositions are **contingent** and logically independent of each other. Their sole function is to represent reality by picturing or mirroring the world. The names in a true elementary proposition correspond with the objects in a corresponding state of affairs, and the arrangement of names in the elementary proposition mirrors the arrangement of objects in the corresponding state of affairs. A list of all the true elementary propositions would be a complete description of reality.

Facts are the obtaining of states of affairs. The world is composed of states of affairs, which are contingent and independent of each other. Any given state of affairs might not have obtained, and any two states of affairs are such that one might have obtained with or without the other. Objects are simple (i.e., have no parts) and necessary. In different possible worlds, different states of affairs obtain, but the very same objects exist in every possible world.

Wittgenstein's theory incurs the following commitments: (a) to the existence of states of affairs and facts; and (b) to a substantial relation of correspondence or sameness of form. The arrangement of names in an elementary proposition mirrors the arrangement of objects in a corresponding state of affairs.

WITTGENSTEIN'S LOGICAL ATOMISM

According to Wittgenstein's *Tractatus*, the world consists of contingent states of affairs, i.e., structured arrangements of objects. Objects are held to be simple (i.e., have no parts), necessary and (hence) **eternal**. Interpreters differ over the nature of simple objects. Some interpreters regard simples as mental items such as sense-data (thus bringing Wittgenstein's atomism closer to Russell's). Others regard Wittgenstein's simples as mind-independent, or even as logical rather than empirical entities. Wittgenstein's atomism yields a theory of possibility: all states of affairs are contingent, and states of affairs are independent of each other. Any given arrangement of objects could have been different. It is essential to objects that they can combine with other objects to form states of affairs. The actual world consists of objects as they are in fact arranged. Possible states of affairs are simply rearrangements of actual objects. Objects are thus held to be common to every possible world (that is, common to every world we can imagine).

Comments on Wittgenstein's Logical Atomism

Following the tradition of his compatriots, Husserl and Meinong, Wittgenstein distinguishes facts from states of affairs, and holds that a fact is the obtaining of a state of affairs. The totality of facts just is the totality of obtaining states of affairs. However, it is not obvious what theoretical gain results from distinguishing between facts and states of affairs. How are we to conceive of non-obtaining states of affairs? Are they abstract entities? Are they non-existent entities?

The alternative view, held by, e.g., Bradley, McTaggart and Russell, dispenses with states of affairs, and regards facts as exemplifications of properties and relations. McTaggart defined a fact as: 'either the possession by anything of a quality, or the connection of anything with anything by a relation'.[2] He gave the following illustration: 'If I say "the table is square" the only thing which can make my assertion true is the fact that the table is square – that is, the possession by the table of the quality of squareness.'[3]

For Wittgenstein, although objects compose states of affairs, facts (the obtaining of states of affairs) are the basic or fundamental **ontological** units. ('The world is the totality of facts, not of things' (1.1).) It is of the essence of an object that it does combine, and can combine, with other objects to form states of affairs. Hence, there could not be a possible world consisting of just one object – any object can exist only in configuration with other objects.

There are no complex facts, only atomic ones. This is because of 4.0312: the **logical constants** are not names and do not stand for objects. The meaning of 'not', 'or' etc., is not some logical object, but is displayed by the individual truth-tables for each constant. If a proposition corresponds to a fact, each element in the proposition must correspond to a counterpart element in the fact (4.04). In which case, a complex proposition such as 'Bill is bald or Fred is fat' cannot correspond to a complex fact, since there is nothing to which the 'or' could correspond. Hence, there can be no complex facts. This is just as well since complex facts – e.g., negative, disjunctive, conjunctive and **conditional** facts – have always been regarded with suspicion. (Russell almost caused a riot when he defended the existence of negative facts to an audience at Harvard.)

Although all facts are atomic, not all propositions are elementary. There are complex propositions, but such propositions are not required for a complete description of the world. Complex propositions are **truth-functions** of elementary propositions, so they need not feature in the inventory of being (4.26). For example, if 'Bill is bald or Fred is fat' is true only because Bill is bald, then that disjunctive truth does not need to be included in a description of reality, provided 'Bill is bald' appears there.

Towards the end of the 1920s Wittgenstein realized that there were serious problems with the *Tractatus* philosophy. One crucial difficult, relevant here, is that states of affairs are not independent of each other. (There was an exactly similar problem for elementary propositions.) The state of affairs of A's being red excludes the state of affairs of A's being green. Since it is impossible for both states to obtain, this undermines the Tractarian idea of states of affairs as independent entities.

Wittgenstein believed, on strictly *a priori* grounds, that language, properly analysed, must decompose into elementary propositions consisting only of names, and that reality must decompose into independent states of affairs consisting only of configurations of simple objects. But in the absence of even the beginning of an analysis, the whole project came to seem chimerical.

Of course, not all friends of facts think of facts as the obtaining of contingent, independent states of affairs composed of eternal, simple objects. Are there objections that might be made against the invocation of facts more generally? We can now turn to the criticisms of one modern opponent of facts, the American philosopher Donald Davidson.

DONALD DAVIDSON (1917–2003)

Donald Davidson was, along with his mentor and major philosophical influence, W.V.O. Quine, one of the most important **analytic** philosophers of the 20th century. He taught at major US universities (Stanford, Princeton, Rockefeller), but spent most of his professional life at Berkeley, from 1981 until his death in 2003. Davidson made seminal contributions to many areas of philosophy, most notably to the philosophy of language, mind and action. He wrote many articles (collected together in *Actions and Events* (1980) and *Truth and Interpretation* (1984)), together with a very accessible posthumously published book *Truth and Predication* (2005). One of Davidson's leading ideas is that Tarski's theory of truth can yield a theory of meaning for natural languages, thus enabling meaning to be reconstructed from purely extensional materials. Davidson is also known for his anomalous monism, which combines the token–token identity of mental and physical events with the denial of psycho-physical laws, and for his sophisticated defence of the thesis that reasons are causes of actions.

• DAVIDSON ON FACTS

Davidson has criticized the correspondence theory of truth because of its commitment to facts. In his posthumously published book *Truth and Predication*, Davidson offers three objections to an ontology of facts.

(i)   One objection is that 'it is a fact that P' is just a variant on saying 'it is true that P' or, indeed, just a variant on saying 'P'. So saying that a true sentence corresponds to the facts is a pseudo-explanation: '"[i]t is a fact that Theatetus sits" is just a wordy way of saying that Theatetus sits."'[4] Davidson's thought is that 'it is a fact that P' and 'it is true that P' are too close together for the former to correspond to, or be explanatory of, the latter.

Two replies can be made. First, facts and truths are not that close together: on, e.g., Wittgenstein's Logical Atomism only basic or elementary truths correspond to facts. Complex propositions do not correspond to facts. Second, if truths are linguistic entities and facts are chunks of extra-linguistic reality, then they are independent, and do not simply collapse into each other.

(ii) Davidson objects that facts have no clear conditions of individuation: 'no one knows how to individuate facts in a plausible way.'[5] Davidson's thought is presumably that unless we can say under what conditions the fact that A is the same as, or different from, the fact that B, we have no real idea what facts are. However, there seems no reason why a facts theorist cannot give the following clear and straightforward account of the identity and individuation of facts: the fact that a is F is the same as the fact that b is G just if a = b and the property of being F = the property of being G.

(iii) The third objection Davidson cites, which was presented explicitly by Alonzo Church, but credited to Frege and C.I. Lewis, is known as the Slingshot argument. It is a somewhat technical argument and its conclusion is that there is only one fact.[6] This would be a devastating conclusion for the friends of facts, since there is assumed to be a multiplicity of facts. However, the Slingshot argument assumes that definite descriptions are referring terms, not disguised **quantifiers**. Given the plausibility of Russell's theory that descriptions are disguised quantifiers (see Chapter 3), we can reasonably reject the Slingshot argument.

In sum, there may be problems with logical atomism and the correspondence theory of truth, but their commitment to facts has not been shown to be one of them.

• TRUTHMAKER THEORY

An interesting development in recent metaphysics has been the elaboration and defence of truthmaker theory. A lucid and forceful advocate has been the leading Australian philosopher David Armstrong.[7] Armstrong defends the most extreme version of truthmaker theory, truthmaker maximalism:

(TM) Every truth has a truthmaker.

The motivation for (TM) is clear enough: if a sentence or proposition is true there must be something in virtue of which it is true. That in virtue of which a proposition is true is its truthmaker. The phrase 'true in virtue of' is standardly understood as **entailment**. That is, if X is the (or a) truthmaker for P, then the existence of X necessitates the truth of P:

(TN) X exists → P.

That is, necessarily, if X exists, P is true.

A third principle is required in light of the possibility that two or more distinct truths may have the same truthmaker. For example, suppose that P is true and Q false. Then the truthmaker for P will also be a truthmaker for (P or Q). Since P entails (P or Q), this suggests the following general principle:

(EP) If X is a truthmaker for P, and P entails R, then X is a truthmaker for R.

This principle allows that different truths can have the same truthmaker. Conversely, it is also possible for one truth to have many truthmakers. For example, if P and Q are both true, then (P or Q) will have two truthmakers.

The key question is whether a version of truthmaker theory combining (TM), (TN) and (EP) is defensible.

Three preliminary points

(i)   In the case of some true propositions, the truthmaker will not be a fact but an object. For example, the truthmaker for 'Obama exists' is arguably Obama, not any fact involving him. But for many other truths, facts will be truthmakers. Thus consider the truth that Bill is bald. What could make this true? Not Bill; not the property of baldness; nor the set {Bill, baldness}. For one thing, all these candidate truthmakers violate (TN). There are possible worlds containing both Bill and the property of baldness in which Bill is not bald – any world in which Bill is hairy but others are bald.

The only plausible candidate truthmaker is the fact that Bill is bald. This fact is not just the set of Bill and baldness but the unified entity of Bill's being bald. It is an addition to being over and above its constituents. The fact that Bill is bald satisfies (TN): any possible world containing that fact is a world in which it's true that Bill is bald. The fact necessitates the truth. Consequently, if truth-maker theory is plausible, we will have a reason to believe in facts.

(ii) There is the following crucial difference between truthmaker theory and Witt-genstein's Logical Atomism (or correspondence theories of truth in general). In truthmaker theory there is no commitment to the idea that a truth and its truth-maker must share a common form or structure. This is plain from the obser-vation that objects can sometimes be truthmakers, and from the observation that truths with different logical structures (e.g., 'P' and 'P or Q') can have the very same truthmaker. But even in the case of 'Bill is bald' and the fact that Bill is bald, there is no requirement that the internal structure of the truth mirror the internal structure of the fact. All that is required is that the fact necessitate the truth.

(iii) Note also that correspondence is a **symmetric** relation (if x corresponds to y, y corresponds to x), whereas truthmaking is an **asymmetric** relation (if X makes true P, P does not make true X). The key relations of truthmaker theory and correspondence theory are quite different.

TRUTHMAKER THEORY

Although there are different versions of truthmaker theory, its driving intuition is that every truth (i.e., true sentence or proposition) must have a truthmaker. If P is true there must be some worldly item in virtue of which P is true. In a slogan: truth supervenes on being. If two possible worlds differ in their truths, there must be some difference in being: the worlds must differ in respect of their objects or their properties and relations. Various kinds of entities may be truthmakers. In some cases, e.g., positive true existential claims such as 'Obama exists', objects will be truthmakers. In the case of other truths, e.g., 'Socrates is wise', facts seem the only plausible candidates to be truthmakers. The central task facing truthmaker theory is to show that and how every truth has a truth-maker. Problem cases include general truths, negative truths and **modal** truths (truths of possibility and necessity).

• PROBLEMS WITH TRUTHMAKER THEORY

But should we accept truthmaker theory? Are (TM), (TN) and (EP) jointly plausible theses? These questions have received a lot of attention in recent discussions, but I will focus on two problem cases: general truths and negative truths (though, as we shall see, they may turn out to be different aspects of the same problem).

The problem of general truths

Consider any accidentally true generalization of the form *all As are Bs* (e.g., all the balls in this urn are red), where there are only finitely many As. Given (TM), this truth must have a truthmaker. We might think that the truthmaker is an irreducibly general fact, as Russell once did. But since we have no clear idea of general facts, they are best avoided if possible.

There is one seemingly obvious way of avoiding commitment to general facts. The truth that all As are Bs, it might be said, is logically equivalent to the conjunction of singular truths: this A is B; that A is a B, etc. Each of these truths is made true by an atomic fact, and we can think of their conjunction as made true by the relevant set of atomic facts (set S). Since the conjunction is equivalent to the general truth 'all As are Bs' we can – by (EP) – take the truthmaker for the general truth to be the set S. We thus avoid the need to postulate any general facts.

However, there is a problem with this line of reasoning. The conjunction 'this A is B; that A is B ...' is not logically equivalent to 'all As are Bs'. For consider a possible world in which all the actual As exist and are Bs, but in which there are additional As which are not Bs. (This relies on the plausible assumption that there might have been more As than there actually are.) In that world the conjunction is true, yet it is not true that all As are Bs. So the conjunction and the general truth cannot be logically equivalent. For the same reason, set S does not necessitate the truth of 'all As are Bs'. The world just imagined contains that set of facts, yet not all As there are Bs.

Armstrong is aware of this problem and posits a 'totality fact' (the fact that there are no more As) which together with set S necessitates the truth of 'all As are Bs'.[8] This gets round the problem, but the trouble is that a totality fact is a negative fact, and we have a strong intuition that there cannot be negative facts, that everything that exists is positive. This brings us on to the second problem – finding truthmakers for negative truths. If we could solve this problem, we might vindicate Armstrong's solution to the problem of general truths.

The problem of negative truths

Some truths are positive (e.g., 'Obama is President'), but many are not (e.g., 'there are no unicorns'). By (TM) all truths must have truthmakers, including negative truths. But surely the world cannot contain negative truthmakers – for what would a negative fact be like? How could there be such a mysterious thing?

Some negative truths will be entailed by positive truths, and – by (EP) – those negative truths will have positive facts as truthmakers. Thus suppose it is true that Fred is fat. Then it is true that Fred is not thin. But since 'Fred is not thin' is entailed by 'Fred is fat', the truthmaker for the positive truth is also a truthmaker for the negative truth. However, not all negative truths are entailed by positive truths – e.g., there are no unicorns. What are the truthmakers for negative truths of this kind?

Armstrong has a relatively economical way of dealing with such truths. The combination of all positive facts plus the totality fact <there are no more positive facts> is a truthmaker for 'there are no unicorns' and all other negative truths. Thus we do not need to postulate a plethora of negative facts. But, as noted earlier, a totality fact is a negative fact, and thus an affront to common sense. Truthmaker theory, it seems, cannot avoid commitment to negative facts.

Stephen Mumford recently proposed an ingenious solution.[9] Truthmaker theory will not need to postulate negative facts if there are no negative truths. That is Mumford's claim – there are no negative truths; hence no threat to (TM). Of course, in a 'loose and popular' sense there are negative truths (e.g., 'there are no unicorns'). Mumford's idea is that in the 'strict and philosophical' sense there are no negative truths, merely falsehoods. So when regimenting ordinary language for the purposes of doing metaphysics T(~p) (it's true that not-p) should be represented as F(p) (it's false that p). F(p) simply indicates that p lacks a truthmaker. Since there are no negative truths, truthmaker theory avoids commitment to negative facts.

Mumford's solution is not problem-free:

(i)   It might be thought that there is not much daylight between Mumford's line and giving up (TM). In the latter case, one denies that negative truths have truthmakers; in Mumford's case, one excludes negative truths from the category of truths, thus remaining faithful to the letter of (TM). Is there much difference between these two strategies?

(ii) It is natural to suppose that F(p) implies TF(p) (if it's false that p, then it's true that it's false that p). But Mumford cannot acknowledge anything of the form TF(p). If he did, then, by (TM), TF(p) would have to have a truthmaker, and that could only be a negative fact (the fact that p lacks a truthmaker). So Mumford denies that F(p) implies TF(p). But this denial is implausible, even incoherent: how can it be false that there are unicorns without its being true that it's false?

Clearly, then, there are problems facing truthmaker theory. Nonetheless, truthmaker theory remains a fruitful research program and may yet yield a good reason to embrace facts.

• CONCLUDING REMARKS

We have covered a lot of difficult ground in this chapter. We looked at two theories – Logical Atomism and truthmaker theory – which are committed to facts. Though neither theory is without its difficulties, facts deserve a place in any serious metaphysics.

• STUDY QUESTIONS

- What are facts?
- What is the leading idea of Wittgenstein's Logical Atomism?
- What are the main problems facing Logical Atomism?
- What is the motivation behind truthmaker theory?
- Do general truths and negative truths have truthmakers?

• ANNOTATED FURTHER READING

R. White, *Wittgenstein's Tractatus Logico-Philosophicus* (London: Continuum, 2006). A short and readable introduction to Wittgenstein's early work.

D. Davidson, 'True to the Facts', reprinted in his *Inquiries into Truth and Interpretation* (Oxford: Clarendon Press, 1984), pp. 37–55. Difficult material, but a useful critique of facts.

D. Davidson, *Truth and Predication* (London: Harvard University Press, 2005). An accessible introduction to issues surrounding truth and facts.

D.M. Armstrong, *Truth and Truthmakers* (Cambridge: Cambridge University Press, 2004). A lucid statement of truthmaker theory, and a forthright examination of the problems it faces.

• INTERNET RESOURCES

Kevin Mulligan, and Fabrice Correia, 'Facts', *The Stanford Encyclopedia of Philosophy* (Winter 2008 Edition), ed. Edward N. Zalta, URL = <http://plato.stanford.edu/archives/win2008/entries/facts/>.

L. NathanOaklander, (2005), 'Negative facts', *Routledge Encyclopedia of Philosophy*, ed. E. Craig. London: Routledge. Retrieved May 03, 2010, from http://www.rep.routledge.com/article/N118.

Alex Oliver, (1998), 'Facts', *Routledge Encyclopedia of Philosophy*, ed. E. Craig. London: Routledge. Retrieved May 03, 2010, from http://www.rep.routledge.com/article/N021

Ian Proops, 'Wittgenstein's Logical Atomism', *The Stanford Encyclopedia of Philosophy* (Fall 2008 Edition), ed. Edward N. Zalta, URL = <http://plato.stanford.edu/archives/fall2008/entries/wittgenstein-atomism/>.

Thomas Wetzel, 'States of Affairs', *The Stanford Encyclopedia of Philosophy* (Fall 2008 Edition), ed. Edward N. Zalta, URL = <http://plato.stanford.edu/archives/fall2008/entries/states-of-affairs/>.

• NOTES

1. L. Wittgenstein, *Tractatus Logico-Philosophicus*, trans. D.F. Pears and B.F. McGuinness (London: Routledge & Kegan Paul, 1961).

2. J.M.E. McTaggart, *The Nature of Existence* (Cambridge: Cambridge University Press, 1921) Vol. 1, No. 10, p. 11.
3. *Ibid.*, p.10.
4. D. Davidson, *Truth and Predication* (London: Harvard University Press, 2005), p. 126.
5. *Ibid.* p.126.
6. *Ibid.*, pp. 127–30. See the discussion of the Slingshot Argument in Mulligan, Kevin, Correia, Fabrice, 'Facts', *The Stanford Encyclopedia of Philosophy* (Winter 2008 Edition), ed. Edward N. Zalta, URL = <http://plato.stanford.edu/archives/win2008/entries/facts/>.
7. See his *Truth and Truthmakers* (Cambridge: Cambridge University Press, 2004).
8. *Ibid.*, Ch. 6.
9. 'Negative Truth and Falsehood', *Proceedings of the Aristotelian Society*, 107 (2007), pp. 45–71.

12

˙truth

• INTRODUCTION

In John 18:37, Jesus describes his mission: '[I] came into the world ... to bear witness to the truth; and all who are on the side of truth listen to [my] voice'; to which Pilate famously replied, 'What is truth?' (John 18.38). Pilate may have intended his question rhetorically, as one which can have no answer. But many philosophers have attempted to answer it, and it is perhaps the most famous question in philosophy. In this chapter we look at a range of theories of truth and objections to them.

Theorists divide into two camps: those who think truth is a theoretically interesting property, and those who deny this. In the former camp are correspondence theorists, coherence theorists and verificationists or anti-realists. In the latter camp, are so-called deflationists about truth (such as F.P. Ramsey and Paul Horwich). There are also primitivists about truth, such as G.E. Moore, who hold that truth is a simple, indefinable property. There are a number of versions of each of these theories.

A further point of difference concerns the choice of the bearers of truth and falsity. Candidate truth-bearers include sentences, propositions and beliefs, and it can sometimes matter which candidate is selected. These candidates typically have various functions: they represent the world to be a certain way; they are what is true or false; they are what is believed or disbelieved, necessary or **contingent**, etc.

THEORIES OF TRUTH

Correspondence, coherence and anti-realist theories of truth all hold that there is an essence or nature to truth, discoverable by *a priori* reflection. On these theories, truth is correspondence to the facts, coherence with other beliefs, or knowability (understood as in principle decidability), respectively. There are powerful objections to each of these theories. Recoil from theories of this sort leads in either of two directions. Some hold that truth is a simple indefinable property, about which nothing philosophically illuminating can be said. Others hold that truth is not a genuine property at all. Of course, we should believe only truths if we want successfully to engage with the world, but the claim that p is true adds nothing to the assertion that p. On some views, we could dispense entirely with the concept of truth and lose nothing of cognitive significance.

• CORRESPONDENCE THEORIES

The correspondence theory of truth is not simply a reformulation of the oft-heard equivalence "P' is true **if and only if** P'. Nor is it merely a restatement of Aristotle's common sense dictum that 'to say of what is that it is, or of what is not that it is not, is true' (*Metaphysics*, 1011b25). The correspondence theory goes beyond these platitudes. The key idea underlying all versions of the correspondence theory is that a truth-bearer (typically taken to be a sentence or proposition) is true just in case it corresponds to some worldly entity distinct from the truth-bearer, and false just in case it fails to correspond to any such entity.

Alternatve versions of the correspondence theory differ over how to understand 'worldly entity' and 'correspondence'. Worldly entities can be facts, objects, properties, events, and these in turn can be understood in various ways. 'Correspondence' has traditionally been understood to require a structural similarity between some privileged subset of basic or elementary truths and appropriate worldly entities. But 'correspondence' has also been understood less stringently, requiring only a pairing between a truth and a worldly item. J.L. Austin recommends the latter conception of 'correspondence', regarding the former as committing 'the error of reading back into the world the features of language'.[1]

A classic version of the correspondence theory finds expression in the **Logical Atomism** of Wittgenstein's *Tractatus*. Wittgenstein takes the worldly items to be facts and takes correspondence to require that the arrangement of elements (names) in an elementary proposition mirror the arrangements of elements (objects) in the corresponding state of affairs. Arguably, any weaker understanding of correspondence, such as Austin's, fails to distinguish the correspondence theory from truthmaker theory. (See Chapter 11 for discussion and criticism of Logical Atomism and truthmaker theory.)

Wittgenstein held that there is a class of true elementary propositions, and only these propositions correspond to atomic facts. Non-elementary or complex propositions (such as the disjunction 'Bill is bald or Fred is fat') are truth-functions of elementary propositions (such as 'Bill is bald'), and thus all true propositions are made true by atomic facts. (Complex propositions are **truth-functions** of elementary propositions just if the truth-value of a complex proposition is fixed entirely by the truth-values of its contained elementary propositions. The truth-value of 'Bill is bald or Fred is fat' is determined by the truth-values of 'Bill is bald' and 'Fred is fat'.)

So the classic correspondence theory holds: (i) elementary propositions have the same structure as states of affairs; (ii) complex propositions are truth-functions of elementary propositions.

Problems with the correspondence theory

Each commitment is problematic. Are there any elementary propositions, as (i) assumes? According to Wittgenstein, elementary propositions are logically independent of each other. For any two elementary propositions, it must be possible for both to be true together, both false, and one true and the other false.

Consider the proposition that A is red and the proposition that A is green. Plainly they cannot be true together; hence these propositions are not elementary.[2] But if they're not elementary, what propositions of English are elementary? In the *Tractatus* Wittgenstein thought that natural language sentences, properly analysed, would reduce to logically independent elementary propositions. But he offered no examples of these fully analysed elementary propositions, nor did he indicate any method by which we might uncover them.

Commitment (ii) is doubly problematic. First, it requires that there be a genuine class of elementary propositions. Second, even given that assumption, (ii) is implausible. Natural languages contain many complex truths (e.g., 'Necessarily 2 = 2 = 4', 'Fred believes that Bill is bald', 'if Mary had been driving, we would have been killed' etc.) which seem not to be truth-functions of their contained propositions or of any other elementary propositions.[3]

Frege's objections to the correspondence theory

In his famous essay 'The Thought' Frege offers two objections to the correspondence theory.

(a) A correspondence ... can only be perfect if the corresponding things coincide and are, therefore, not distinct things. ... But then there can be no complete correspondence, no complete truth.'[4]

However, (a) is assertion rather than argument. The correspondence theorist should just insist that there is a workable notion of correspondence that falls short of identity. But Frege's comments do point towards another theory, recently revived: the identity theory of truth. According to this theory, endorsed at various times by Moore and Russell, a true proposition is identical to a fact.

Since facts are composed of objects, properties, relations, etc., the identity theorist must take true propositions to contain objects, properties and relations as constituents. The proposition that Obama is American contains Obama and the property of being an American as constituents. This conception of true propositions is controversial, and would be rejected by Frege and his followers. Fregean 'thoughts' are **abstract** objects composed only of abstract senses.

Further, what does the identity theorist say about false propositions? Clearly, they are not identical to facts since there are no 'false facts'. But then what are they identical to? What are they? Any answer to this question would have the odd consequence that true propositions have one nature, false ones another.

(b)   The correspondence theory generates a **vicious regress**. In order to decide whether T is true, i.e., whether T corresponds to some fact F, we should have to decide whether 'T corresponds to F' is true, i.e., whether there is some fact to which 'T corresponds to F' corresponds, and so on. Frege concludes: 'So the attempt to explain truth as correspondence collapses. And every other attempt to define truth collapses too.'[5]

If I look out the window and see that grass is green, I can thereby know that the sentence 'grass is green' is true. I do not need to verify whether '"grass is green" corresponds to the fact that grass is green" is true – I already know that it's true. There is a logical regress exploiting the iterability of 'is true': if 'P' is true, then 'P is true' is true, and if '"P is true" is true' then ... . But this is normally held to be a paradigm example of a harmless regress precisely because one does not have to verify later members of the series in order to verify earlier ones. So Frege's objection lapses.

• COHERENCE THEORIES

Correspondence theorists tend to be **realists**: they think of facts as mind-independent entities. (But not always. McTaggart accepted a version of the correspondence theory and was an idealist.) The coherence theory of truth has traditionally been associated with idealism. Some coherence theorists have held that truth comes in degrees and that only the 'whole complete truth' is really true. Another feature of the coherence theory is that beliefs, not sentences or propositions, are taken to be truth-bearers.

According to the coherence theory, a belief is true if and only if it is part of a coherent set of beliefs. Since a system of beliefs can be more or less coherent, individual beliefs can be true to a higher or lower degree. A belief is more true the more it coheres with other beliefs. On some views, only a maximally coherent set of beliefs is completely true. The coherence theory is considered idealist since it holds that the truth of a belief consists not in correspondence to external reality but in fit with other beliefs. On some versions of the theory, reality consists in systems of beliefs.

How should we understand 'coherence' and why is the theory formulated in terms of beliefs rather than sentences or propositions? 'Coherence' is normally held to mean at least consistency – only a logically consistent set of beliefs (held by a person at a time) can be coherent. But consistency is not enough for coherence. In a coherent set of beliefs each belief supports, reinforces or explains other beliefs. Such support can be deductive (e.g., where one belief entails another) or inductive (e.g., where taking on a new belief simplifies or best explains one's prior beliefs).

It is clear now why, on the coherence theory, neither propositions nor sentences can be bearers of truth. Propositions may stand in relations of **entailment** or consistency to other propositions, but propositions do not explain other propositions. The proposition that it is raining does not explain the proposition that the ground is wet (similarly for sentences); but my belief that it is raining does explain, along with other beliefs I hold, why I believe that the ground is wet. So beliefs are best suited to be truth-bearers for the coherence theorist.

Two problems now come to the fore. (i) Surely there are many truths which no one will ever believe. How can the coherence theorist make sense of this evident possibility? (ii) If truth is a matter of coherence between held beliefs, what rules out two sets of beliefs counting as equally coherent, where one set contains the belief that P while the other set contains the belief that not-P? Both beliefs would count as true, yet no tenable theory of truth can allow incompatible beliefs to be true (or even true to the same degree). The coherence theorist could retreat to relativism about truth in response to this objection: the belief that P is not true *simpliciter*, but true-for-subject-S (while the belief that not-P is true-for-S*). But this is not our conception of truth – e.g., disagreement would be impossible on the relativist view.

• ANTI-REALISM

In *Language, Truth and Logic*, A.J. Ayer defended the verificationist theory of meaning.[6] According to this doctrine, any meaningful proposition is either **analytic** (true in virtue of meaning) or empirical (which Ayer understood as 'in principle verifiable by sense-experience'). Thus, e.g., 'all spinsters are female' is analytic; 'there is an elephant in the next room' is empirical since in principle verifiable by sense-experience, i.e., there is a finite number of steps one could take which would result in experiences that either supported the sentence or counted against it. On this view, a declarative sentence is meaningless if it fails to express a proposition which is either analytic or empirically verifiable.

Ayer's criterion of meaningfulness proved impossible to formulate in any precise and satisfactory way. Various formulations of the criterion admitted sentences that should clearly be excluded. The criterion is anyway implausible. Intuitively, a sentence such as 'everything (including ourselves) is doubling in size', despite being neither analytic nor empirically verifiable, is perfectly meaningful.

A.J. AYER (1910–1989)

Sir Alfred Jules ('Freddie') Ayer was educated at Eton and Christ Church, Oxford. He became Grote Professor at University College, London, before taking up the Wykeham Chair of Logic at Oxford in 1959. A colourful and controversial figure, he had a wide circle of friends and divided much of his time between Oxford and London. One of the leading British philosophers of the last century, fame came early in life with the publication of *Language, Truth and Logic* in 1936. The propositions of metaphysics were declared meaningless since neither analytic nor empirically verifiable. Propositions of logic and mathematics, indeed all *a priori* propositions, were counted analytic. Ethical sentences, such as 'torture is wrong', which are neither analytic nor empirically verifiable, were deemed meaningful by virtue of expressing attitudes or emotions, rather than by stating ethical facts. Though Ayer later modified the stark doctrines of his early work, he never relinquished his **empiricist** outlook.

However, the idea that there is a connection between truth and verifiability was rehabilitated by Michael Dummett in a series of articles from the 1960s onwards, and the resulting theory is known as anti-realism.[7] Earlier disputes between realists and their opponents often turned on whether, e.g., numbers, universals, material objects, etc., existed and, if they did, whether they were mind-dependent. Dummett's thought was that these disputes can more fruitfully be discussed, even resolved, by examining the notion of truth appropriate to statements about such objects. Realism could then be understood as the view that the truth of statements in a disputed class was subject to no epistemic or verificationist constraints. Anti-realism stands in opposition to such a view. Though far from dogmatic, Dummett's sympathies lie with the anti-realist.

Two case studies: arithmetic and other minds

(i) Arithmetic

According to the Dummettian anti-realist, we have no conception of 'what it would be for ... a statement to be true independently of the sort of thing we have learned to recognize as establishing the truth of such a statement'.[8] In the case of, e.g., a mathematical statement, the canonical method of verification is proof. Consider Goldbach's famous, and currently undecided, conjecture that every even number is the sum of two primes. This conjecture is one for which we currently have neither proof nor counterexample. According to Dummett we are therefore not entitled to think of Goldbach's conjecture as either true or false. Anti-realists thus reject the principle of **bivalence** (the principle that every statement is true or false). We would only be entitled to regard Goldbach's conjecture as either true or false if we were actually in possession of a proof or a counterexample (or, at least, in possession of a method which would be guaranteed to lead, in a finite series of steps, to a counterexample).

(ii) Other minds

An example involving the attribution of mental states to other people also illustrates the anti-realist position. Suppose we ask of the recently deceased Jones whether he was brave or not. As it happens, Jones led a sheltered life at a university and never encountered danger. We have no direct evidence for 'Jones was brave' and no direct evidence for 'Jones was not brave'. Nor do we have any indirect or auxiliary evidence (e.g., other character traits which normally accompany bravery or the lack of it). In that case, says Dummett, we cannot regard 'Jones was brave' as either true or false.

THE UNTESTED JONES

Professor Jones led a sheltered life in his university town, ensconced in his book-lined set, rarely venturing out to those parts of town where ruffians and footpads hold sway. Jones never encountered danger. He was never threatened or attacked himself, nor did he witness such outrages being committed against others. Nothing in his behaviour provides evidence for the truth of 'Jones was brave' or for the truth of 'Jones was not brave'. Nor are we in possession of any method that will enable us to decide the issue by a mechanical procedure in a finite time. Let us suppose, further, that no relevant evidence will turn up in the future. Then, says Dummett, it's not the case that 'Jones was brave' is either true or false. The realist, in contrast, says that 'Jones was brave' is a precise, unambiguous declarative sentence of English, true if Jones had the quality of braveness, false otherwise. Since Jones either possessed that quality or not, 'Jones was brave' is either true or false, even if we have no idea which. Our evidence for a statement is one thing, its truth or falsity another.

The realist response

Dummett's opponent, the bivalence-endorsing realist, holds that 'Jones was brave' must '*be* either true or false, since the man's character ... must either have included the quality of bravery or lacked it'.[9] Dummett complains that 'only a philosophically quite naïve person would adopt a realist view of statements about character.'[10] However, the realist view of the matter is intuitive. We think of psychological characteristics, such as bravery or anger, as lying behind and giving rise to behaviour. Our mental states are not to be identified with our behaviour, but rather cause our behaviour. Further, we have no difficulty with the idea that, due to self-control or to favourable external circumstances, a person may have a certain psychological quality even though it never shows up in his behaviour.

The anti-realist position on Goldbach's conjecture is similarly unintuitive. We have no apparent difficulty with the idea that either every even number is the sum of two primes or not, even if we can never decide the issue. Anti-realism about arithmetical statements must be distinguished from **error theory** about arithmetic – i.e., the view that there are no numbers and hence that all arithmetical statements are false. If numbers exist, and if the predicates 'even' and 'sum of two primes' suffer from no vagueness or ambiguity, how can it fail to be the case that either each of the infinitely many even numbers is the sum of two primes or that at least one is not?

Anti-realism disproved?

Whatever the plausibility of Dummett's verdict on these and other examples (e.g., statements about the past for which we have no evidence for or against and no prospect of acquiring such evidence), there is a powerful argument against the coherence of anti-realism. The argument was originally due to F.B. Fitch, and was first published in 1963.[11]

It is a consequence of anti-realism that there are no unknowable truths. If there were unknowable truths, then a statement could be true, even though there was no possibility of us ever coming to recognize it as true. It is precisely such independence of mind from reality that the anti-realist wishes to outlaw. Realism, in contrast, is quite consistent with the existence of unknowable truths. Thus the anti-realist is committed to the following principle:

> (KP) For all statements p, if p is true, it is possible to know p.

Although the anti-realists cannot countenance unknowable truths, they must allow that some truths are unknown. This is simply an expression of our lack of omniscience. The anti-realist, like anyone else, must allow that there are many truths which we will never know (e.g., because no one has bothered to gather the evidence or because it would take too long for humans to gather it). Thus, for the anti-realist, although there are no unknowable truths, there are many unknown truths. Let q designate such an unknown truth.

Fitch's proof proceeds as follows (where 'K' stands for 'it is known that ...' and '~' stands for 'not'):

(1) q and ~Kq; so

(2) Possibly K(q and ~Kq); so

(3) Possibly (Kq and K~Kq); so

(4) Possibly (Kq and ~Kq); so

(5) (KP) is false; so

(6) Anti-realism is false.

Premise (1) is an assumption everyone accepts. It expresses our lack of omniscience. Premise (2) says that it's possible to know (q and ~Kq). (2) follows from (1) by (KP) (substituting 'q and ~Kq' for 'p'). Premise (3) follows from (2) by the principle that knowledge distributes over conjunction, together with a possibility principle. The former principle says that anyone who knows a conjunction thereby knows each conjunct: from 'X knows A and B' we may infer 'X knows A' and 'X knows B'. The latter principle says that from 'Possibly R' and 'R entails S' we can infer 'Possibly S'.

Premise (4) follows from (3) by the principle that knowledge implies truth: from 'X knows that A' we may infer the truth of 'A'. This principle is regarded as essential to knowledge. Knowledge, unlike belief, is **factive** (I can have false beliefs, but no one can have 'false knowledge'). The move from (3) to (4) also requires an application of the possibility principle.

But (4) is false – nothing of the form 'Possibly A & ~A' can ever be true. Hence, some earlier premise or principle must be false. Premise (1) is unassailable; the possibility principle and the principles that knowledge distributes over conjunction and that knowledge implies truth seem undeniable. Hence the source of the contradiction must be (KP). So (KP) is false, and since anti-realism entails (KP), anti-realism is false. The proof establishes the initially surprising result that if some truths are unknown then not all truths are knowable.[12]

REALISM, IDEALISM, ANTI-REALISM

For many, realism is the default view of the world. According to traditional realists, mountains, continents and planets exist independently of us. Had we not existed, they would still have existed, and if we were to cease to exist, they would still exist. In contrast, idealists hold mountains, continents, planets, etc., to be collections of ideas. To be is to be perceived (*esse est percipi*) – either by a human mind or a divine one. According to the idealist, were there no minds, there would be no mountains, continents or planets. Dummett's anti-realism is intended to occupy a position midway between realism and idealism. The world is not independent of us, since statements about the external world cannot be unrecognizably true. But the existence of the planets does not depend on their being perceived by some mind. The planets would still have existed even if there had been no minds.

• DEFLATIONISM

A common feature of all the previous theories is that truth is a theoretically interesting property – e.g., corresponding to the facts, cohering with other beliefs, being knowable/decidable. But in recent years a range of theories have been advanced – which we can group together under the label 'deflationism' – according to which there is no interesting property of truth. These theories differ in various ways, but they all share one basic idea: truth has no metaphysical nature.

The paradigm example of a deflationist approach to truth is the redundancy theory, first outlined, though not unequivocally endorsed, by Frege, and later championed by F.P. Ramsey. In 'The Thought' Frege wrote:

> It is worthy of notice that the sentence 'I smell the scent of violets' has the same content as the sentence 'it is true that I smell the scent of violets'. So it seems, then, that nothing is added to the thought by my ascribing to it the property of truth.[13]

In his article 'Facts and Propositions' Ramsey writes:

> Truth and falsity are ascribed primarily to propositions. The proposition to which they are ascribed may be either explicitly given or described. Suppose first that it is explicitly given; then it is evident that 'It is true that Caesar was murdered' means no more than that Caesar was murdered, and 'It is false that Caesar was murdered' means that Caesar was not murdered.[14]

Frege and Ramsey are both making the point that, at least in cases where the proposition or thought is explicitly given, the presence of the word 'true' adds nothing to the meaning of what is said. Thus 'it's true that roses are red' says no more than that roses are red.

What of a case where the proposition is described rather than explicitly given? An example might be 'The last thing the Pope said is true'. We can capture the content of this sentence, without using the word 'true', by rendering it as: for all propositions P, if P was the last thing the Pope said, then P. Since occurrences of 'true' are everywhere eliminable, there is no property of truth whose nature needs to be investigated.

The key doctrine of deflationism is that the so-called equivalence schema:

(ES) for all propositions p, <p> is true if and only if p

exhausts the content of 'true' (where '<p>' names a proposition). Note that to accept (ES) is not to endorse a correspondence theory of truth.

Two problems for deflationism

(i) We have a firm intuition that truth supervenes on being (see the discussion of truthmaker theory in Chapter 11). That is, if <p> is true, it is true in virtue of p. We thus seem committed to the following **asymmetric** explanatory principle:

   (EX) for all propositions p, <p> is true because p, and not vice versa.

   For example, we think <grass is green> is true because grass is green. We don't think: grass is green because <grass is green> is true. (EX) seems as much a platitude about truth as (ES), yet (ES) by itself cannot account for (EX). The **biconditional** relation in (ES) ('if and only if') is symmetric and hence cannot explain the asymmetry of explanation encapsulated in (EX). At the very least, this shows that (ES) cannot be the whole story about truth, as deflationists maintain.

(ii) Language abounds with vague terms. Terms such as 'many', 'few', 'red', bald', tall', 'small', etc., are all vague. There is much controversy over how to characterize vagueness, but one standard view is the following. The vagueness of, e.g., 'bald', consists in the fact that the predicate clearly applies to some people, clearly fails to apply to others, and neither clearly applies not clearly fails to apply to yet others. This shows up in our attributions of truth-values to sentences containing 'bald'.

Bill, as we know from elsewhere in this book, has not a single hair on his head. The sentence 'Bill is bald' is true. Pamela Anderson has flowing blonde locks – 'Pamela is bald' is false. But consider Bill's brother, Ben. Ben is a borderline case of baldness: he has some hair, but really not much. On one standard account, 'Ben is bald' is neither true nor false. Vague terms can feature in sentences which are true, false, or indeterminate (i.e., neither true nor false).

Consider any indeterminate proposition, s. Does s satisfy (ES)? A biconditional such as (ES) is true just if both sides of the 'if and only if' have the same truth-value. Consider the following instance of (ES):

(S) <s> is true if and only if s.

If s is indeterminate, then presumably '<s> is true' is false. In that case the left-hand side of (S) (<s> is true) is false while the right-hand side (s) is indeterminate (hence not false). Since the two sides of (S) fail to have the same truth-value, (S) cannot be true. But (S) is an instance of (ES), so (ES) is not true.

This is a problem for deflationists, though it should be said there is no shortage of responses. For example, Tim Williamson has recently defended an account of vagueness as ignorance of sharp cut-off points rather than as indeterminacy in truth-value. On his view, 'Ben is bald' is either true or false, we just don't – indeed can't – know which.[15]

• CONCLUDING REMARKS

We have looked, albeit briefly, at some of the leading theories of truth, and found them all open to objection. The objections to the meaty theories of truth – correspondence, coherence and anti-realist theories – are powerful. It may be that some variety of deflationism can be defended against the objections ranged against it, but the debate is still very much open.

• STUDY QUESTIONS

- What is the correspondence theory of truth?
- Why be a coherence theorist?
- How would you characterize Dummett's anti-realism?
- Is it plausible to think that 'Jones was brave' can fail to be true or false?
- How might an anti-realist reply to Fitch's proof?
- How would you defend deflationism against the two objections in the text?

• ANNOTATED FURTHER READING

A.J. Ayer, *Language, Truth and Logic* (Harmondsworth: Penguin, 1976). Ayer's book is the classic statement of logical positivism. This doctrine can usefully be seen as an ancestor of anti-realism.

M.A.E. Dummett, 'Realism' and 'The Reality of the Past', in his collection *Truth and Other Enigmas* (Cambridge, Mass.: Harvard University Press, 1978), pp. 145–66 and pp. 358–75. Both articles are quite difficult, but 'Realism' is the more accessible of the two.

D. Edgington, 'The Paradox of Knowability', *Mind*, Vol. 94 (1985). A useful if high-level discussion of Fitch's paradox.

G. Frege, 'The Thought' (trans. A.M. and Marcelle Quinton), *Mind*, Vol. 65 (1956), pp. 289–311. Reprinted in P.F. Strawson (ed.), *Philosophical Logic* (Oxford: Oxford University Press, 1977), pp. 1–17. A beautifully clear outline of Frege's philosophy of language, truth and reality.

P. Horwich, *Truth* (Oxford: Blackwell, 1990). A clear and thorough defence of minimalism (deflationism) about truth.

J. McDowell, 'Criteria, Defeasibility and Knowledge', *Proceedings of the British Academy*, 68 (1982), pp. 455–79. Reprinted in J. Dancy (ed.), *Perceptual Knowledge* (Oxford: Oxford University Press, 1988). A nice critique of the epistemological underpinnings of anti-realism. Clearly written, if demanding.

• INTERNET RESOURCES

B. Brogaard and J. Salerno (2004), 'Fitch's Paradox of Knowability', *The Stanford Encyclopedia of Philosophy* (Summer 2004 edition), ed. Edward N. Zalta. Retrieved 31 May 2006 from <http://plato.stanford.edu/archives/sum2004/entries/fitch-paradox>.

E. Craig (1998), 'Realism and Antirealism', *Routledge Encyclopedia of Philosophy*, ed. E. Craig. Retrieved 31 May 2006 from <http://www.rep.routledge.com/article/N049>.

Richard L.Kirkham, (1998), 'Truth, Correspondence Theory of', *Routledge Encyclopedia of Philosophy*, ed. E. Craig. London: Routledge. Retrieved May 31, 2010, from http://www.rep.routledge.com/article/N064.

Marian David, 'The Correspondence Theory of Truth', *The Stanford Encyclopedia of Philosophy* (Fall 2009 Edition), ed. Edward N. Zalta, URL = <http://plato.stanford.edu/archives/fall2009/entries/truth-correspondence/>.

A. Miller (2005), 'Realism', *The Stanford Encyclopedia of Philosophy* (Fall 2005 edition), ed. Edward N. Zalta. Retrieved 31 May 2006 from <http://plato.stanford.edu/archives/fall2005/entries/realism>.

Daniel Stoljar, and Nic Damnjanovic, 'The Deflationary Theory of Truth', *The Stanford Encyclopedia of Philosophy* (Fall 2009 Edition), ed. Edward N. Zalta, URL = <http://plato.stanford.edu/archives/fall2009/entries/truth-deflationary/>.

James O. Young, 'The Coherence Theory of Truth', *The Stanford Encyclopedia of Philosophy* (Fall 2008 Edition), ed. Edward N. Zalta, URL = <http://plato.stanford.edu/archives/fall2008/entries/truth-coherence/>.

• NOTES

1. J.L. Austin, 'Truth', in his *Philosophical Papers*, ed. J.O. Urmson and G.J. Warnock (Oxford: Oxford University Press, 1970), p.125.
2. See *Tractatus*, 6.3751.
3. As Dan Stoljar has pointed out to me, although 'necessarily p' is not a truth-function of p, it could be a truth-function of other atomic sentences. For example, if 'necessarily p' was understood as the conjunction 'in w1, p & in w2 p & in w3 p & ...' then it would be a truth-function of atomic sentences (provided that each conjunct is either atomic or reducible to atomic sentences, and provided that the conjunction is finite).
4. G. Frege, 'The Thought', trans. A.M. and Marcelle Quinton, *Mind*, 65 (1956), p. 291.
5. *Ibid.*, p. 291.
6. A.J. Ayer, *Language, Truth and Logic* (Harmondsworth: Penguin, 1976).
7. See, e.g., M.A.E. Dummett, 'Realism' and 'The Reality of the Past', in his collection *Truth and Other Enigmas* (Cambridge, Mass.: Harvard University Press, 1978), pp. 145–65 and 358–74.
8. 'The Reality of the Past', *op. cit.*, p. 362.
9. 'Realism', *op. cit.*, p. 150.
10. *Ibid.*, p. 150.
11. F. Fitch, 'A Logical Analysis of Some Value Concepts', *The Journal of Symbolic Logic*, Vol. 28 (1963), pp. 135–42.
12. For doubts about the proof, see, e.g., D. Edgington, 'The Paradox of Knowability', *Mind*, Vol. 94 (1985), pp. 557–68, and J. Kvanvig, 'The Knowability Paradox and the Prospects for Anti-Realism', *Nous*, Vol. 29 (1996), No. 4, pp. 481–501.
13. Frege, *op. cit.*, p. 293.
14. F. Ramsey, 'Facts and Propositions', *Proceedings of the Aristotelian Society*, Supplementary Volumes, Vol. 7 (1927), p. 157.
15. See T. Williamson, *Vagueness* (London: Routledge, 1994).

˙glossary

a priori

Designates the way in which a sentence or statement is known. A sentence is known *a priori* just if it is known through reason and reflection alone. 'All bachelors are men' is known *a priori*; 'water boils at 100 degrees Celsius' is not. Though related, the notion of the *a priori* should be distinguished from the notions of necessity (truth in all possible situations) and analyticity (truth in virtue of meaning). Knowledge which is not *a priori* is *a posteriori* or empirical.

abstract

This word has many different meanings, but two are important for our purposes. (i) When philosophers describe universals or numbers as abstract objects, they mean abstract in the sense of not in space or time. (ii) When trope theorists describe tropes as abstract particulars, they mean abstract in the sense of 'fine', 'partial', or 'diffuse'. A billiard ball's redness trope exists in space and time. The adjective 'abstract' can also mean formal or mathematical. The noun 'abstraction' also has a number of meanings – e.g., considering only some aspects of a whole.

accidental/essential

This distinction derives from Aristotle. The properties of an object can be divided into those that are accidental and those that are essential. If F is an accidental property of x, then, though x is F, x might not have been F. If G is an essential property of x, then x could not but have been G. In possible worlds talk, if F is an accidental property of x, there are possible worlds in which x exists but is not F; if G is an essential property of x, there are no worlds in which x exists but is not G.

analytic

A sentence is said to be analytic when it is true (or false) in virtue of meaning alone. Examples include 'all bachelors are men', 'all spinsters are women', 'all triangles have three sides'. A non-analytic or synthetic sentence is true (or false) in virtue of its meaning and the worldly facts. Examples include 'all bachelors wear trousers', 'all spinsters are miserable', 'triangles are my favourite geometric object'. There is also the use of 'analytic' to mean critical or rigorous – e.g., as in 'analytic philosophy'.

antecedent

In a conditional of the form 'if P then Q', P is the antecedent (and Q is the consequent).

asymmetric
A relation R is asymmetric just if aRb implies not(bRa). The relation 'is the father of' is asymmetric: if Ron is the father of Dick, Dick is not the father of Ron.

biconditional
The relation 'if and only if' expresses the biconditional, so-called because it is the conjunction of two conditionals. 'P if and only if Q' means 'if P then Q and if Q then P' and is true just if P and Q have the same truth-value.

bivalence
The principle that every statement is either true or false. Bivalence should be distinguished from the Law of Excluded Middle which says, for all p, either p or not-p. One could reject Bivalence but accept Excluded Middle. The principle of Bivalence has been questioned in the case of statements containing empty singular terms and vague predicates, and on anti-realist grounds.

causal loop
A causal loop involves both backwards and forwards causation (e.g., A causes B causes C causes D causes A). Some philosophers think that causal loops are paradoxical, and so impossible. Others think they are oddities but still metaphysically possible.

concrete
A concrete object is one existing in space or time. The objects we see around us exist in space and time; souls and symphonies exist in time only. Not all spatio-temporal objects are made of matter – e.g., shadows and holes are concrete but not made of matter. There is also a more colloquial use of 'concrete' meaning familiar or life-like – e.g., as in 'can you give a concrete example?'

conditional
A conditional is any sentence of the form 'if P then Q', where P is the antecedent and Q the consequent.

contingent
A sentence is contingent if it is true in some possible circumstances (or possible worlds) and false in others. Thus 'it rained in Edinburgh on 1 January 2006' is contingent: it is true, but it might have been false. A sentence is non-contingent or necessary if it is either true in every possible circumstance or false in every possible circumstance. We also acknowledge non-propositional entities (e.g., you, me, the spatio-temporal universe) as contingent. Any contingent being might not have existed. In possible worlds talk, contingent beings exist in some worlds but not in all.

counterfactual conditional
A counterfactual conditional is a conditional with a false antecedent which states what would have been the case had the antecedent been true. Thus, I may not throw a brick at the window, but we can still truly say: if I had thrown a brick at the window, the window would have smashed. We all use and understand counterfactuals, but

there is much dispute about their underlying logic. David Lewis, for example, holds that 'if A had happened, B would have happened' is true just if the most similar A-world to the actual world is also a B-world.

criteria of identity

A criterion of identity for (concrete) Fs tells us what the identity over time of Fs consists in, and hence tells us what changes an F can survive, and what changes destroy an F. It is normally assumed that the criterion of identity for Fs will not presuppose the notion of F-identity. Criteria of identity are thus standardly conceived as reductive in character.

de dicto/de re

This distinction crops up in different areas of philosophy. It is a well-known distinction in the philosophy of possibility and necessity. In a *de dicto* modal sentence such as 'necessarily 2 + 2 = 4', necessity is predicated of a sentence or proposition. In the *de re* sentence 'Socrates is essentially human', a non-propositional object, Socrates, is held to have a property essentially.

deductively valid

An argument is deductively valid just in case its conclusion follows from its premises by truth-preserving rules of inference. If an argument is deductively valid, it is impossible for its premises to be true and conclusion false.

dualism

The word 'dualism' refers to a number of doctrines in philosophy, but I will mention two. In the philosophy of mind, it denotes the view that mind and body are distinct substances or the view that mental and physical properties are distinct. In the metaphysics of properties, it denotes the view that entities are either particulars or universals.

empiricist

The classic empiricist philosophers were Locke, Berkeley and Hume. The central tenet of empiricism is that substantial or worldly knowledge can be gained only via one or more of the five senses. Reason may indeed yield knowledge (e.g., of the *a priori* truths of logic and arithmetic), but such knowledge is not worldly or substantial. Rationalists hold that reason can yield knowledge of the world. An obvious example of a rationalist argument is the Ontological Argument which attempts to prove the existence of God by reason alone.

empty names

These are proper names which lack a referent, such as 'Sherlock Holmes'. The meaning of this name, clearly, cannot be its referent. Maybe the name abbreviates some definite description. But to this view there are many objections. (See S. Kripke, *Naming and Necessity*, for a famous discussion.)

entailment
A statement P entails a statement Q just if it is impossible for P to be true and Q false. The entailment of Q by P thus requires more than the actual truth of P and Q.

epiphenomenalism
A version of dualism about the mind according to which mental events and states are causally impotent. They are caused by physical events and states, but do not themselves cause anything (mental or physical).

error theory
The term 'error theory' has come to mean a theory which holds that a range of sentences in some discourse are false due to lack of appropriate worldly items. An error theorist about arithmetic holds that sentences such as '2 + 2 = 4' are false because there are no numbers. An error theorist in ethics holds that sentences such as 'stealing is wrong' are false because there is no property of wrongness.

eternal
An object is eternal just if it always has existed and always will exist. Eternal objects need not be necessary existents.

factive
A mental state or linguistic operator F is factive just if Fp implies p. Knowledge is factive: if X knows p then p is true. Belief is not factive: X may believe q though q is false.

five-dimensionalism
On one extreme view there are five-dimensional objects composed of individual parts located in different possible worlds. You and your other-worldly counterparts are but world-parts of larger five-dimensional entities, just as (on the perdurantist view) your different temporal parts compose the larger four-dimensional entity that is you.

general term
A general term, such as 'red', 'square' or 'horse', is a term which applies to, or can apply to, more than one object.

if and only if
A sentence of the form 'P if and only if Q' is equivalent to the conjunction 'if P then Q and if Q then P' and is therefore true only when P and Q have the same truth-value. (See entry for biconditional.)

indeterministic
On some theories, quantum phenomena are indeterministic. That is, a certain outcome may be likely but not determined by the past states of the universe together with the laws of nature. Such indeterminism is thought to be a consequence of Werner Heisenberg's uncertainty principle.

indexical

A word is an indexical just in case its reference is determined by the context of its utterance. Thus, an utterance of 'I' is indexical since its reference is determined by the identity of its utterer; an utterance of 'here' is indexical since its reference is determined by the location of its utterer; an utterance of 'now' is indexical since its reference is determined by its time of utterance. 'I', 'here', and 'now' are referring terms, yet have the curious feature of immunity to both reference-failure and misreference.

inhere

On the Platonic/Aristotelian conception of properties as universals, universals inhere in, or are instantiated by, particulars. It is hard to say much about inherence/instantiation, or even to make clear sense of it. This difficulty is one of the motivations behind nominalism.

laws of nature

A standard example of a law of nature is: all metals expand when heated. But what are laws of nature? Some philosophers (Humeans) think that laws of nature are simply well-established regularities. Others (anti-Humeans) think that laws involve some kind of necessity which explains the observed regularities.

Leibniz's Law

The law which states that if A is identical to B then every property of A is a property of B and vice versa. This law must be distinguished from the principle of the identity of indiscernibles: if A and B share all their properties, then A is identical to B.

Logical Atomism

This doctrine was associated with Wittgenstein and Russell in the early part of the 20th century. Although their versions of logical atomism differed, their key idea was that language and reality share a common structure and each decomposes to basic constituents (atoms) under logical analysis.

logical constants

These are logical words – such as 'and', 'or', not', 'if ... then ...' – which allow us to construct complex sentences out of atomic ones. From 'A' and 'B' we can construct, e.g., 'A and B', 'A or B', 'not-A', 'not-B' and 'if A then B'. These constants are held to be truth-functional (though this claim is controversial in the case of 'if ... then ...').

metaphysical necessity/possibility

Necessity grounded in the identity and nature of things. It is necessary for 2 to be even, for water to be H_2O, and for Socrates to be human. These necessities flow from the nature of the number 2, water and Socrates, respectively. Metaphysical possibility is possibility consistent with the nature of an object or natural kind. Thus, given his nature as a human being, Socrates might have been a carpenter, but could not have been a tree.

modal
Pertaining to possibility and necessity. Modal sentences are those of the form: possibly P, necessarily P, A might have been F, A is necessarily G, B can't be G, etc. Modal claims have different strengths depending on the modality in question. Thus 'I can't lift that car' refers to a physical impossibility; 'Socrates might not have been a number' refers to a metaphysical impossibility; 'I can't simultaneously lift and not lift that car' refers to a logical impossibility. There are other modalities too (e.g., legal: 'you can't park there').

natural kind
A natural kind, as the name suggests, is a naturally occurring stuff (gold, water, etc.) or species (tiger, dolphin, etc.). Natural kinds can be contrasted with human-made or artificial kinds (cars, computers, etc.) Kripke claimed that natural kind terms are rigid designators, and that the identity of the kind designated is fixed not by its superficial observable characteristics but by its internal structure. On this view, the empirical discovery that water is H_2O reveals the essence of water.

necessary being
God is traditionally conceived to be a necessary being. That is, God exists and it is impossible that God not exist. In possible world talk, God exists in every possible world.

no action at a temporal distance
Temporal analogue of 'no action at a spatial distance'. To give up the temporal principle is to hold that A at t1 can bring about B at t2 directly, without there being any event(s) after t1 and before t2 sufficient to bring about B.

nominalism
Sometimes understood as the view that there are no abstract objects, it is used here to indicate the range of views opposed to the conception of properties as universals.

numerical identity
This sense of 'identity' is expressed in sentences such as 'Hesperus is Phosphorus', 'Superman is Clark Kent', '$2^2 = 4$'. Each of these sentences concerns just one entity, differently named. Numerical identity conforms to Leibniz's Law. That is, if $A = B$, then every property of A is a property of B and vice versa.

omnipotent
God is held to be all-powerful or omnipotent. That is, God is able to bring about any logically possible state of affairs. Thus, it does not tell against God's omnipotence that He cannot make my table be simultaneously round and square, since this is not a logically possible state of affairs. (Descartes, however, thought that God was not bound by the laws of logic.)

omniscience
God is traditionally held to be all-knowing. That is, for any true proposition p, God knows that p. (But if God is outside time, can He know that it is, e.g., now 4 p.m.?)

ontology
The study of fundamental kinds of things (be they objects, properties, events or facts) and the fundamental relations between those kinds. According to W.V.O. Quine, one's ontological commitments are measured by what one is prepared to quantify over. If and only if I accept 'there are Fs' I am thereby committed to the existence of Fs. 'Ontological' is the adjective meaning 'pertaining to ontology'.

open past
The past is open just if it is possible to bring about/cause/influence the past (in just the way we take ourselves to bring about/cause/influence the future). The possibility of an open past does not imply (absurdly) that it is possible to change the past. It implies only that it is possible to do something now to help make the past what it was. The claim is not that our past is open – for there may be no backwards causal chains in our world – merely that an open past is possible.

over-determination
Over-determination occurs when A and B cause C and where either would have caused C in the absence of the other.

physicalism
Physicalism is the view that the self and its mental states are identical to the physical body and its physical states, respectively.

projection
Projectivism about some property F is the view that we mistakenly take F to be a property of things in the external world, when in fact it is generated by our own minds and projected onto the world. Thus, we may describe a situation as fearful, but it is so only because we react to it in a certain way. Hume is the classic source for projectivism. He wrote that 'the mind has a great propensity to spread itself on external objects' (*Treatise*, 1.3.14).

qualitative identity
Exactly resembling things are qualitatively identical. This sense of 'identical' is expressed in 'A and B are identical twins'. This sentence concerns two people not one. Qualitative identity does not conform to Leibniz's Law: if A and B are identical twins, it is not the case that every property of A is a property of B and vice versa. For example, the twins differ in the exact time of their births and in their subsequent spatial paths.

quantifiers
These are words which tell us what proportion or quantity of things have a certain property. Thus all of the following are answers to the question 'How many Fs are Gs?': all Fs are Gs; some Fs are Gs; most Fs are Gs; many Fs are Gs; a few Fs are Gs; no Fs are Gs, etc. The development of quantificational logic by Gottlob Frege in the 19th century represented a major advance over previous systems of logic.

realism
The term 'realism' has many different meanings in philosophy. The following three are relevant to metaphysics. In one sense, realism is the view that the typical objects of perception (trees, mountains, planets, etc.) are mind-independent entities. Their existence does not depend on the existence of any minds. The opposite of realism in this sense is idealism. In a second sense, made popular by Dummett, realism allows for a complete divorce between truth and knowability. Statements about, e.g., the external world can be true or false whether or not we are able to know them. The opposite of realism in this sense is anti-realism. Finally, realism has also been used to designate the view that properties are universals. The opposite of realism in this sense is nominalism.

reductio
A *reductio* argument is one in which an assumption leads to absurdity, and is thus shown to be false. Hence the Latin: *reductio ad absurdum*.

reductive
Words such as 'reductive' and 'reductionist' are philosophers' terms of art, which have many different meanings. It is no longer thought that a reduction of Fs to Gs requires sentences about Fs to be equivalent in meaning to sentences about Gs. It is enough if truths about Fs can be captured without remainder by truths only about Gs. For example, we reduce committees to individuals if truths about committees (e.g., 'the committee unanimously voted to appoint Smith') can be accounted for by truths about individuals. Modality, time, causation and persons are four areas where reductionist claims have been advanced.

rigid designator
This is a technical term, of great theoretical fecundity, due to Saul Kripke. A singular term is rigid just if it picks out the same object in every possible world in which that object exists. Kripke claimed that proper names are rigid but standard uses of definite descriptions are not. Thus, 'the world's tallest man' is non-rigid since, though it picks out Ivan in this world, it picks out other men in other possible worlds. But a proper name such as 'Obama' does no such thing. To put the idea intuitively: someone other than Ivan might have been the world's tallest man, but no one other than Obama might have been Obama.

singular term
A term, such as 'New York', 'Ron Jeremy', or 'Pluto', whose function is to refer to exactly one object (though it will often be an object which itself has parts).

structural isomorphism
The cases that interest us involve representations (sentences, propositions, etc.) and the states of affairs represented. Wittgenstein thought that the arrangement of names in a fully analysed elementary proposition mirror the arrangement of objects in a corresponding state of affairs. Propositions and state of affairs are thus structurally identical or isomorphic.

substance
We can distinguish three notions of substance. First, we talk of substances as objects of reference or as that which has properties. This is the sense of 'substance' relevant to the realist/nominalist debate. Second, we talk of individual substances (this man, that tree, etc.) conceived as unified entities, entities with a distinctive kind of life, and conceptually independent of other entities. Contrast the dent in my car bonnet. We cannot even think of the dent without thinking of the bonnet of which it is a dent. Third, we also talk of substances in the sense of natural kinds (water, gold, tigers, etc.).

symmetric
A relation R is symmetric just if aRb implies bRa. Thus the relation 'is a brother of' is symmetric: if Bill is a brother of Ben, then Ben must be a brother of Bill.

tensed facts
These are facts expressed using A series terms such as 'past', 'present' and 'future'. A theorists hold that tensed facts are irreducible, yet changing, aspects of temporal reality. B theorists hold that there are no such facts. There are only unchanging tenseless facts, expressible in B series vocabulary.

thought-experiment
A thought-experiment is an imaginary experiment in which, typically, some controversial possibility is made vivid. If someone claims 'necessarily P' they stand refuted if a merely possible case in which not-P can coherently be described. Thus, e.g., if we can coherently describe a possibility in which there is time without change, we refute the claim that time necessarily involves change. Since much philosophy attempts to uncover necessities and possibilities, thought-experiments are an important part of the philosopher's tool-kit.

transitive
A relation R is transitive just if aRb and bRc together imply aRc. Relations which are transitive include being the same height as, being bigger than, etc. Relations which are not transitive include loves, is a neighbour of, looks the same colour as, etc.

truth-function
A complex sentence is a truth-function of its component sentence (or sentences) just if the truth-value of its component sentence (or sentences) fixes the truth-value of the complex sentence. The logical constants of elementary logic ('and', 'or', not', etc.) are truth-functional. Thus: 'P and Q' is a truth-function of 'P' and 'Q'; in contrast, 'Necessarily P' and 'Bob believes that P' are not truth-functions of 'P'.

vicious regress
A vicious regress is one where the truth of one step in the regress depends on the truth of its next step, that step on its next step, and so on without end. The truth of the first step is thus never established. Not all regresses are vicious. The regress 'if "P" is true, then "P is true" is true; if … , etc.' is not vicious. This regress merely exploits the harmless iterability of 'is true'.

'yes or no' answer

There are some questions which do not receive a 'yes or no' answer. For example, if we ask 'Is that chap bald?' of some man who has some hairs on his head, but not many, that question may not receive a 'yes or no' answer. Importantly, it seems that no further factual information would enable us to decide the matter.

˙index